RETURN OF THE BUNNY SUICIDES

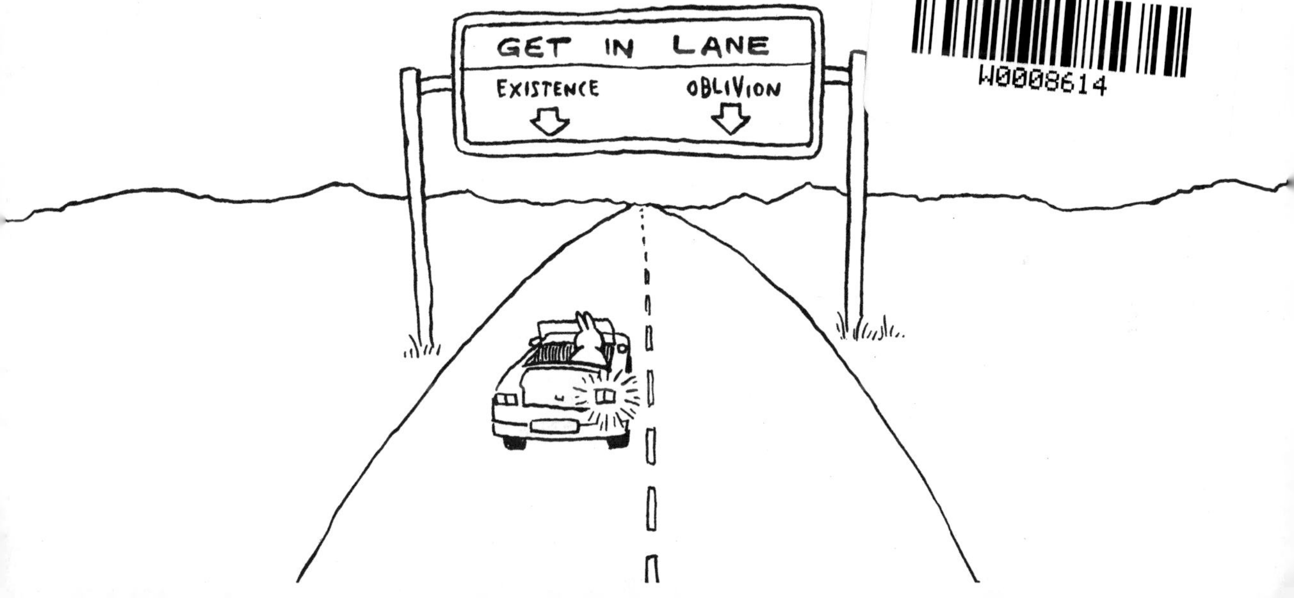
GET IN LANE
EXISTENCE
OBLIVION

VALEAS MUNDUM

ANDY RILEY HAS WRITTEN FOR BLACK BOOKS, TRIGGER HAPPY TV, SO GRAHAM NORTON AND SMACK THE PONY. HE HAS CO-WRITTEN THE BAFTA AWARD-WINNING ROBBIE THE REINDEER, THE RADIO FOUR PANEL GAME THE 99p CHALLENGE AND THE FORTHCOMING DISNEY ANIMATION FEATURE, GNOMEO AND JULIET. HE DRAWS ROASTED, A WEEKLY COMIC STRIP IN THE OBSERVER MAGAZINE. ANDY IS THE AUTHOR OF THE BESTSELLING THE BOOK OF BUNNY SUICIDES.

RETURN OF THE BUNNY SUICIDES

ANDY RILEY

Ⓟ
A PLUME BOOK

PLUME
PUBLISHED BY THE PENGUIN GROUP

PENGUIN GROUP (USA) INC., 375 HUDSON STREET, NEW YORK, NEW YORK 10014, USA
PENGUIN BOOKS LTD, 80 STRAND, LONDON WC2R 0RL, ENGLAND
PENGUIN BOOKS AUSTRALIA LTD, 250 CAMBERWELL ROAD, CAMBERWELL, VICTORIA 3124, AUSTRALIA
PENGUIN BOOKS CANADA LTD, 10 ALCORN AVENUE, TORONTO, ONTARIO, CANADA M4V 3B2
PENGUIN BOOKS INDIA (P) LTD, 11 COMMUNITY CENTRE, PANCHSHEEL PARK, NEW DELHI - 110 017, INDIA
PENGUIN BOOKS (NZ) LTD, CNR ROSEDALE AND AIRBORNE ROADS, ALBANY, AUCKLAND 1310, NEW ZEALAND
PENGUIN BOOKS (SOUTH AFRICA) (PTY) LTD, 24 STURDEE AVENUE, ROSEBANK, JOHANNESBURG 2196, SOUTH AFRICA

PENGUIN BOOKS LTD, REGISTERED OFFICES: 80 STRAND, LONDON WC2R 0RL, ENGLAND

PUBLISHED BY PLUME, A MEMBER OF THE PENGUIN GROUP (USA) INC. THIS IS AN AUTHORIZED REPRINT OF A
HARDCOVER EDITION PUBLISHED BY HODDER & STOUGHTON. FOR INFORMATION ADDRESS
HODDER & STOUGHTON, 338 EUSTON ROAD, LONDON NW1 3BH, ENGLAND

FIRST PLUME PRINTING, FEBRUARY 2005   20 19 18 17 16 15 14 13

BOOKS ARE AVAILABLE AT QUANTITY DISCOUNTS WHEN USED TO PROMOTE PRODUCTS OR SERVICES. FOR INFORMATION PLEASE WRITE TO PREMIUM MARKETING
DIVISION, PENGUIN GROUP (USA) INC., 375 HUDSON STREET, NEW YORK, NEW YORK 10014.

WITH THANKS TO

KEVIN CECIL, ARTHUR MATHEWS, POLLY FABER, CAMILLA HORNBY, TRENA KEATING AND ALL AT PLUME, FREYA AYRES, DAVID AYRES.

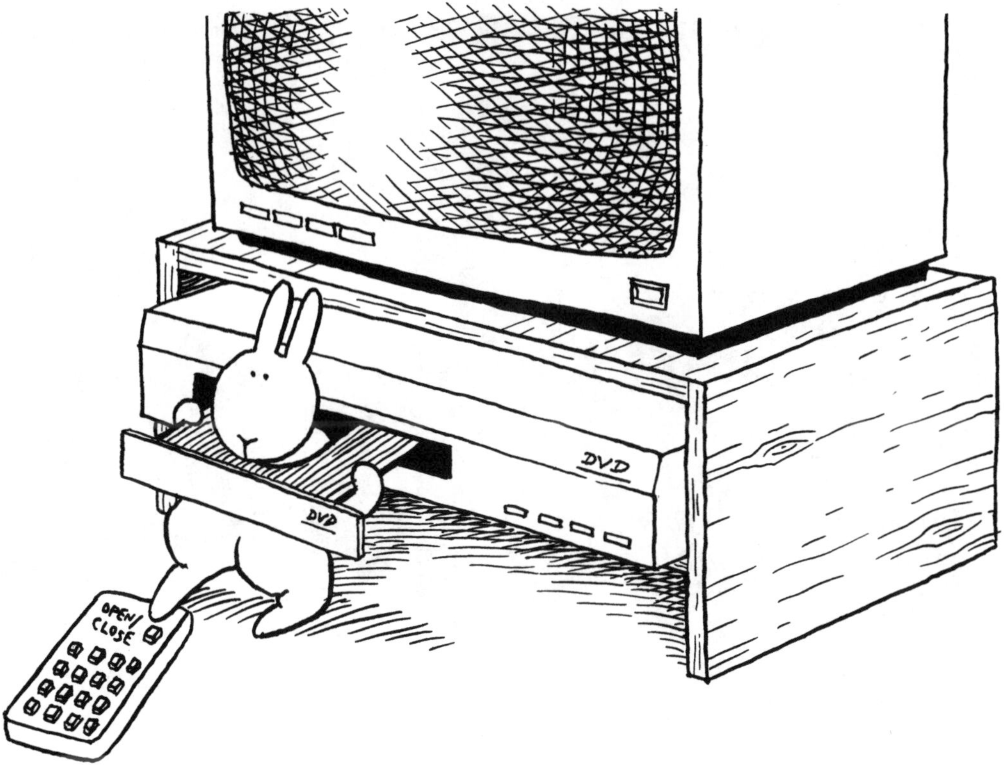
DVD
DVD
OPEN/
CLOSE

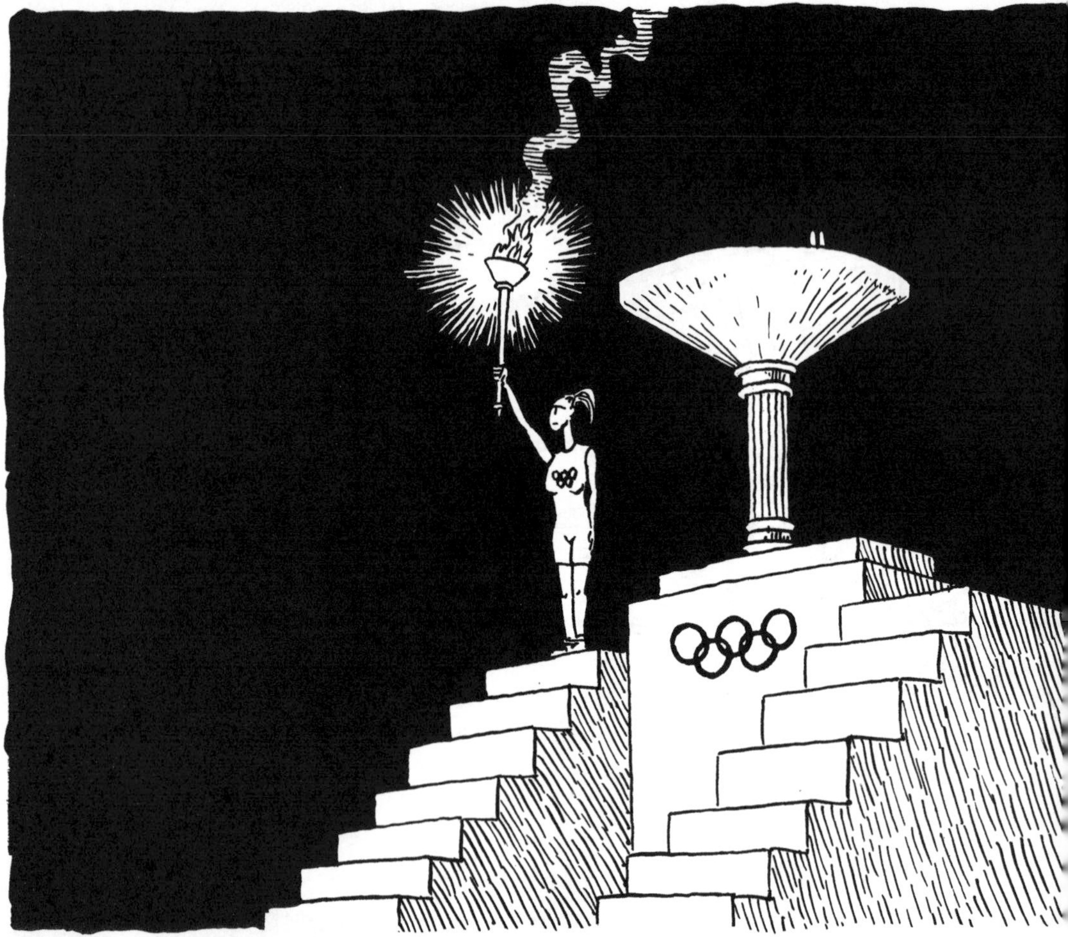

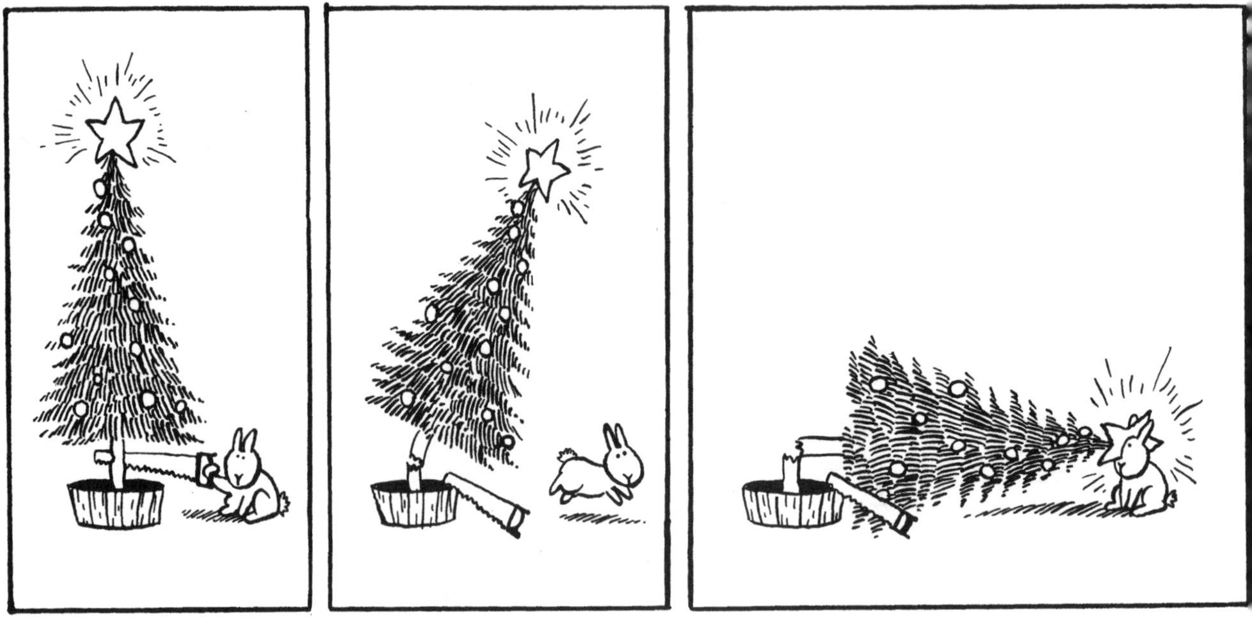

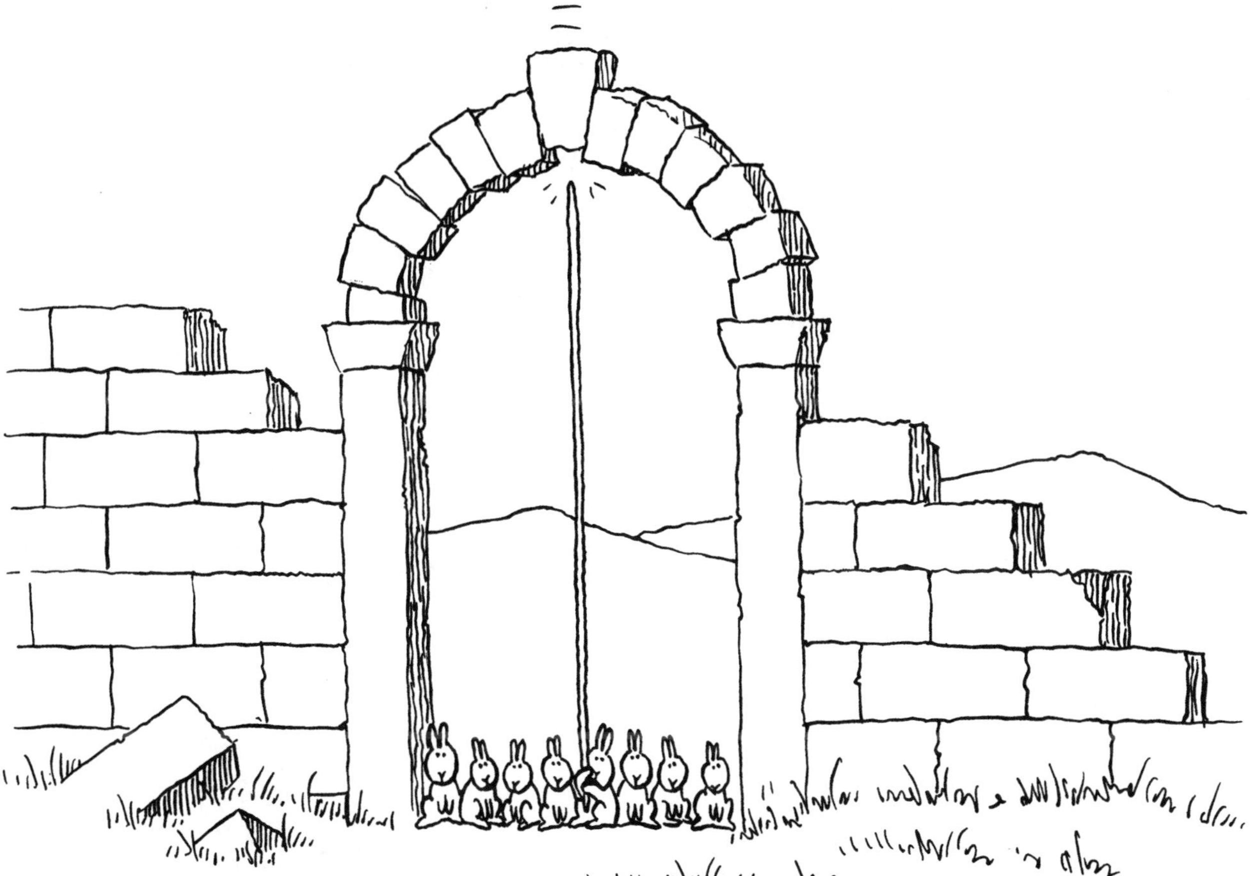

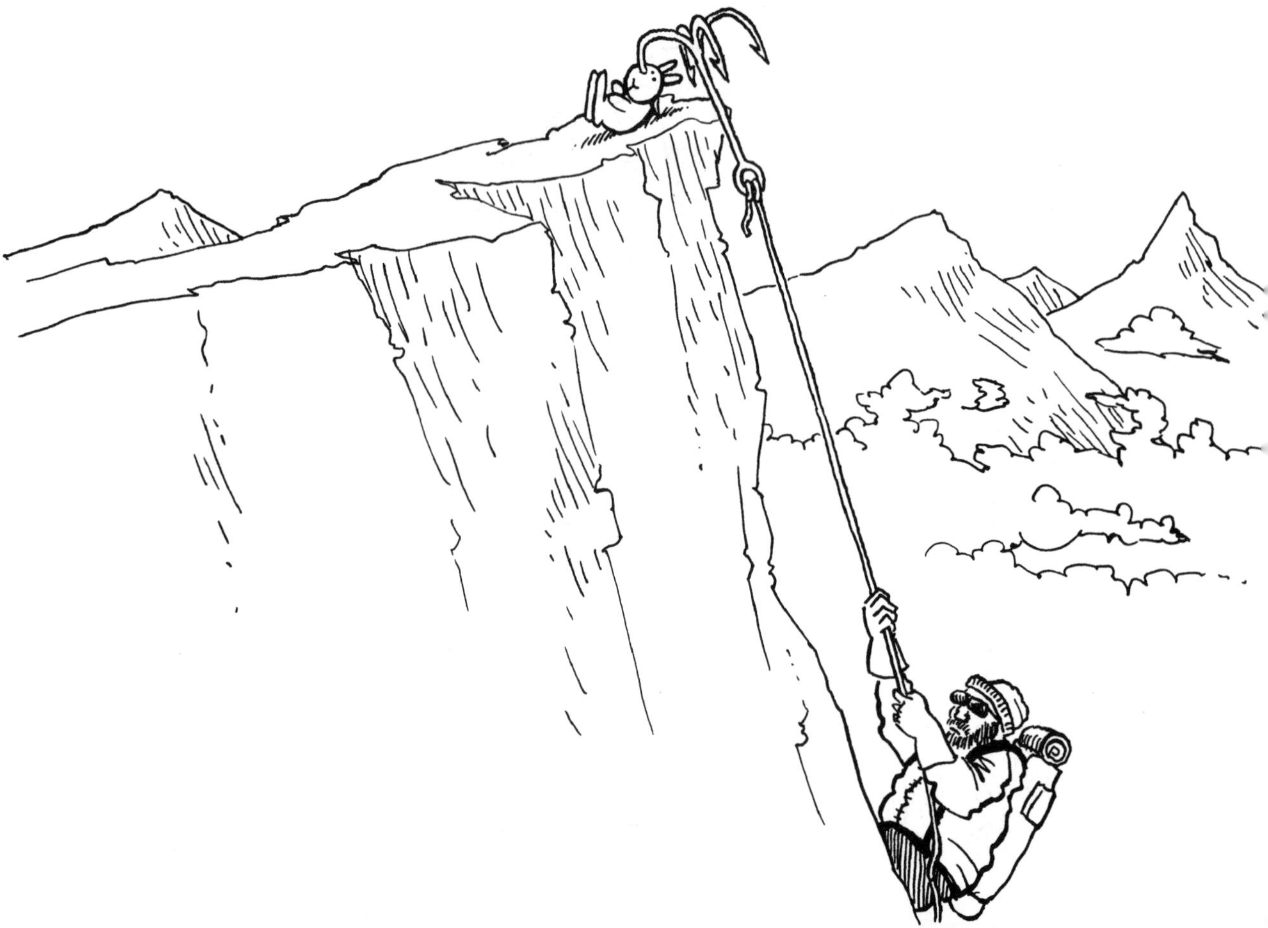

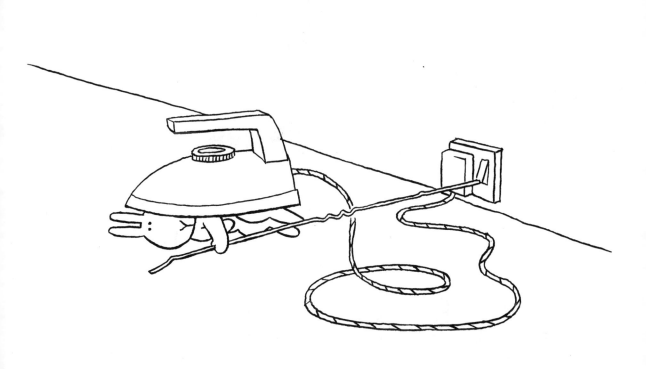

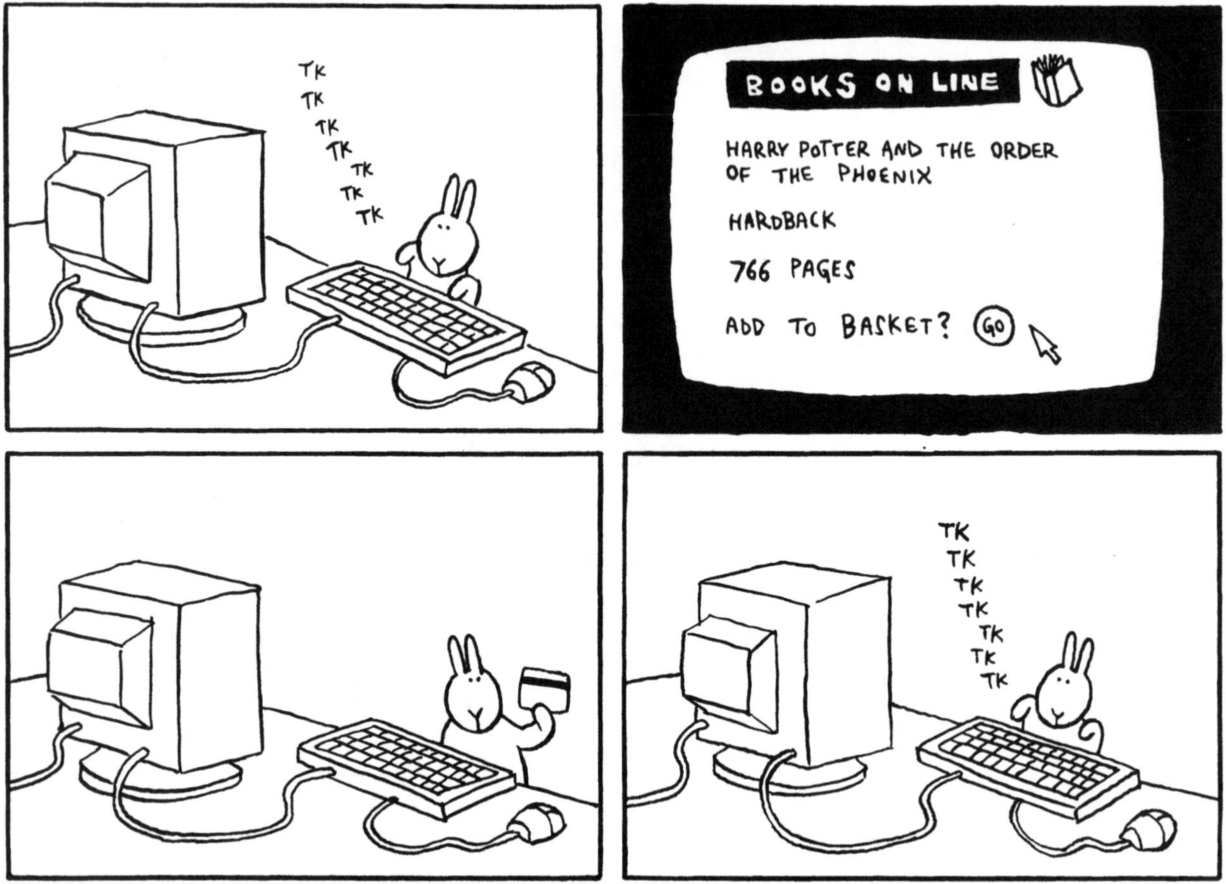
TK
TK
TK
TK
TK
TK
TK
BOOKS ON LINE
HARRY POTTER AND THE ORDER OF THE PHOENIX
HARDBACK
766 PAGES
ADD TO BASKET? GO
TK
TK
TK
TK
TK
TK
TK

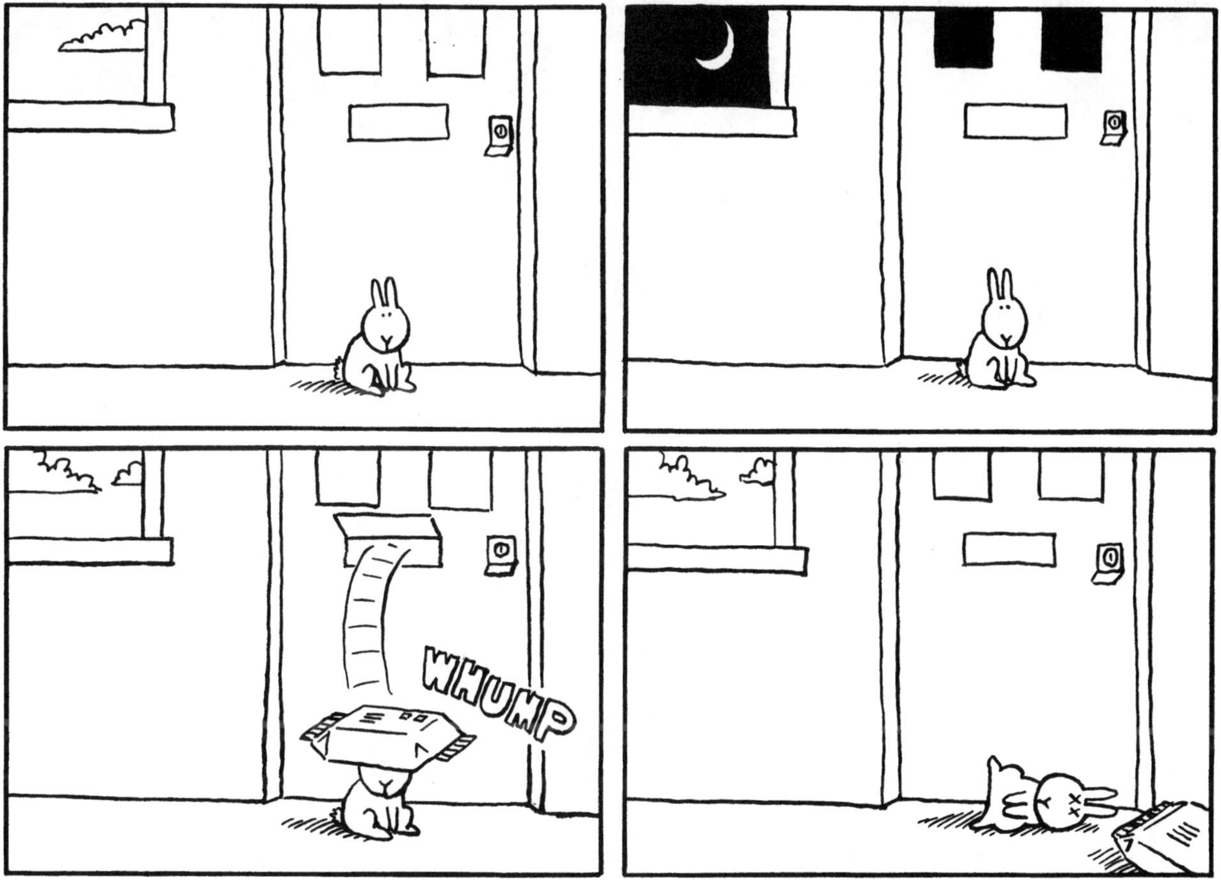
WHUMP

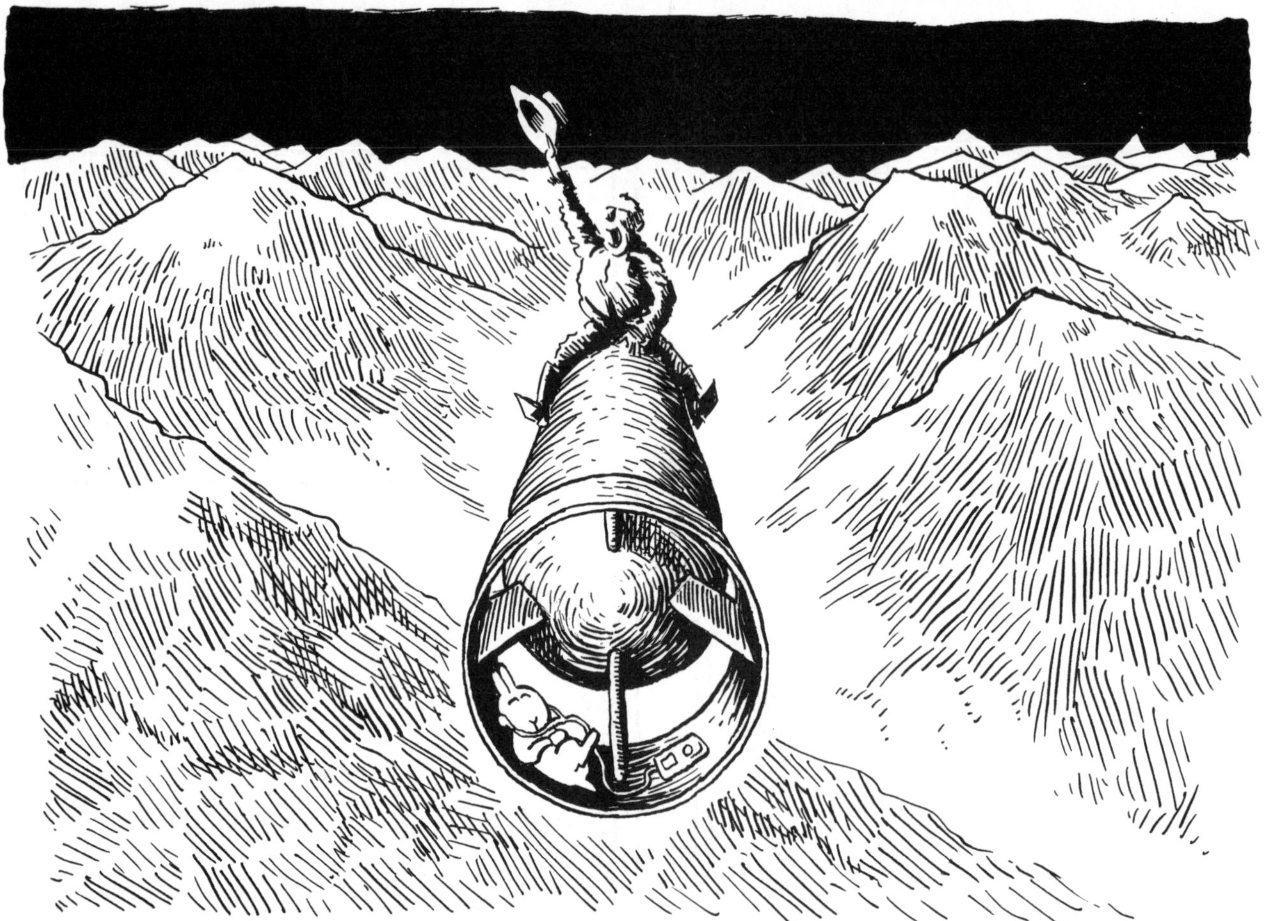

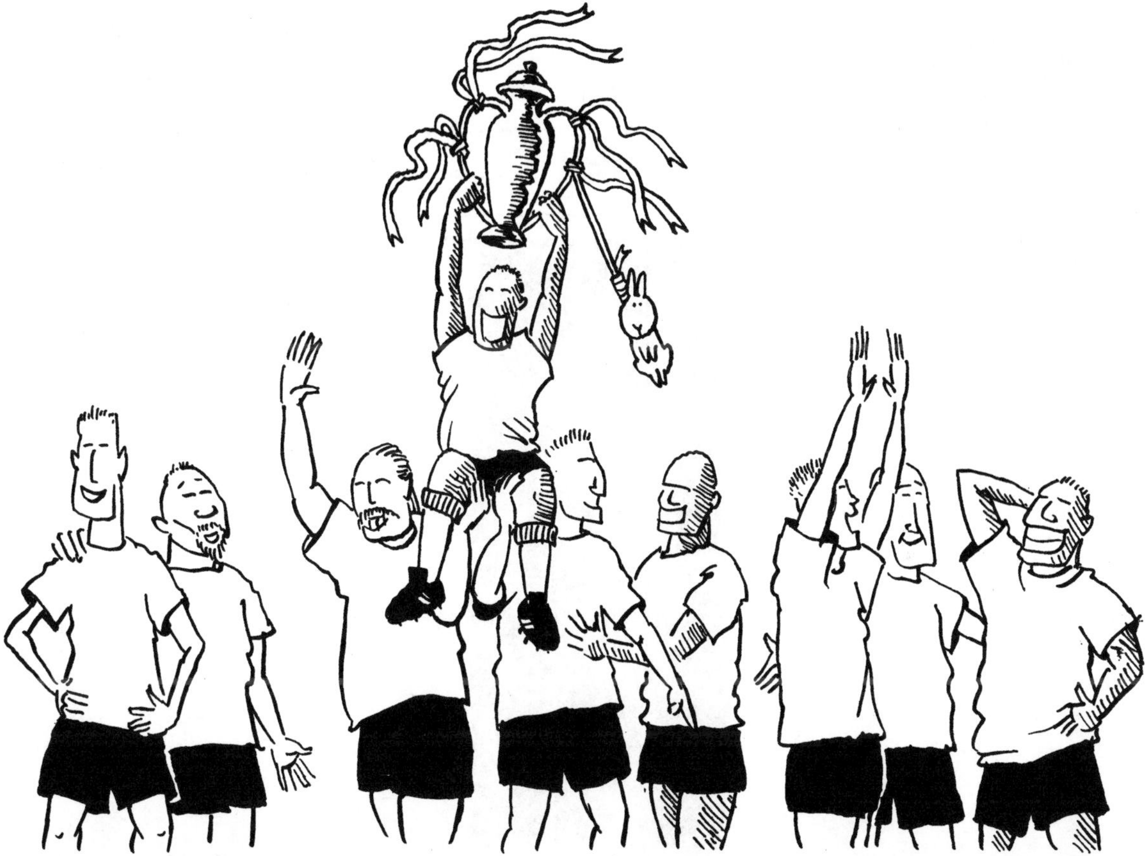

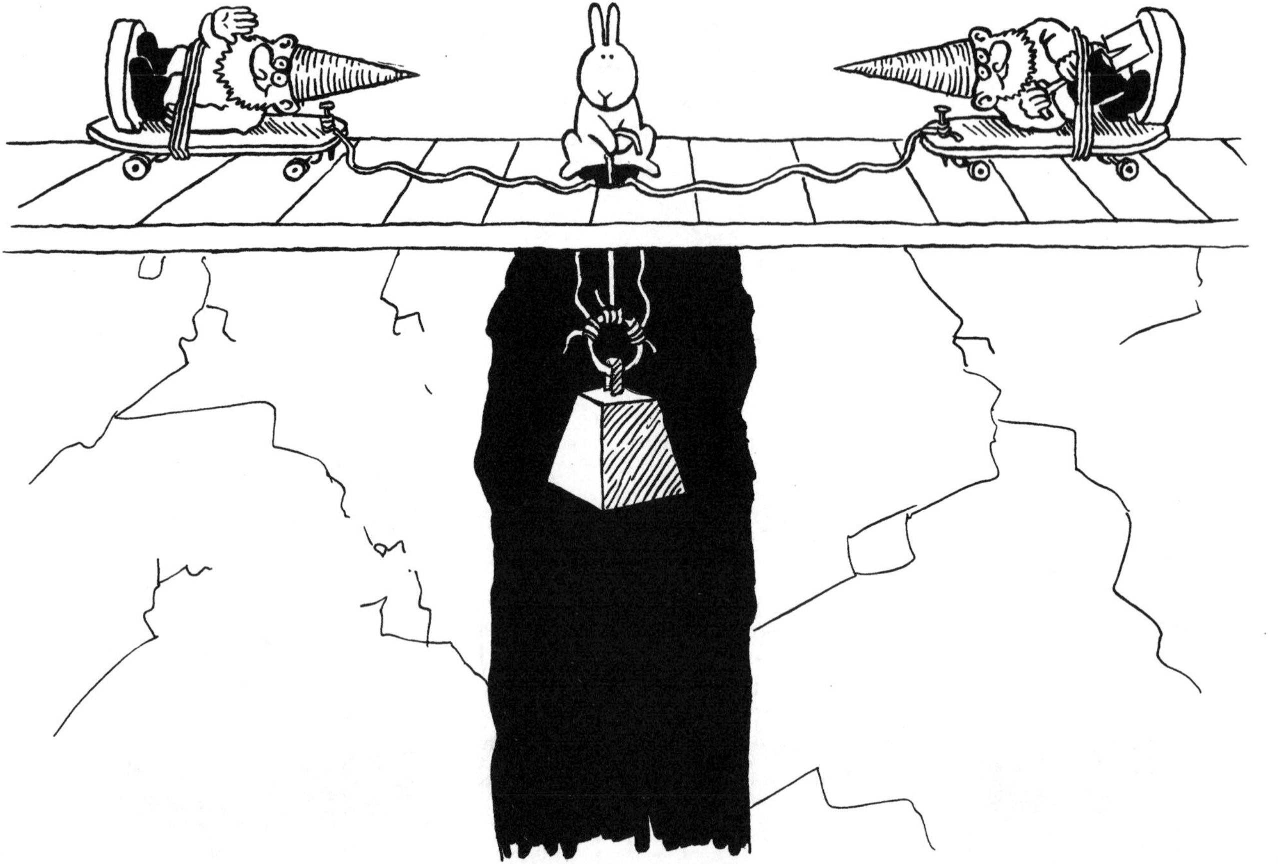

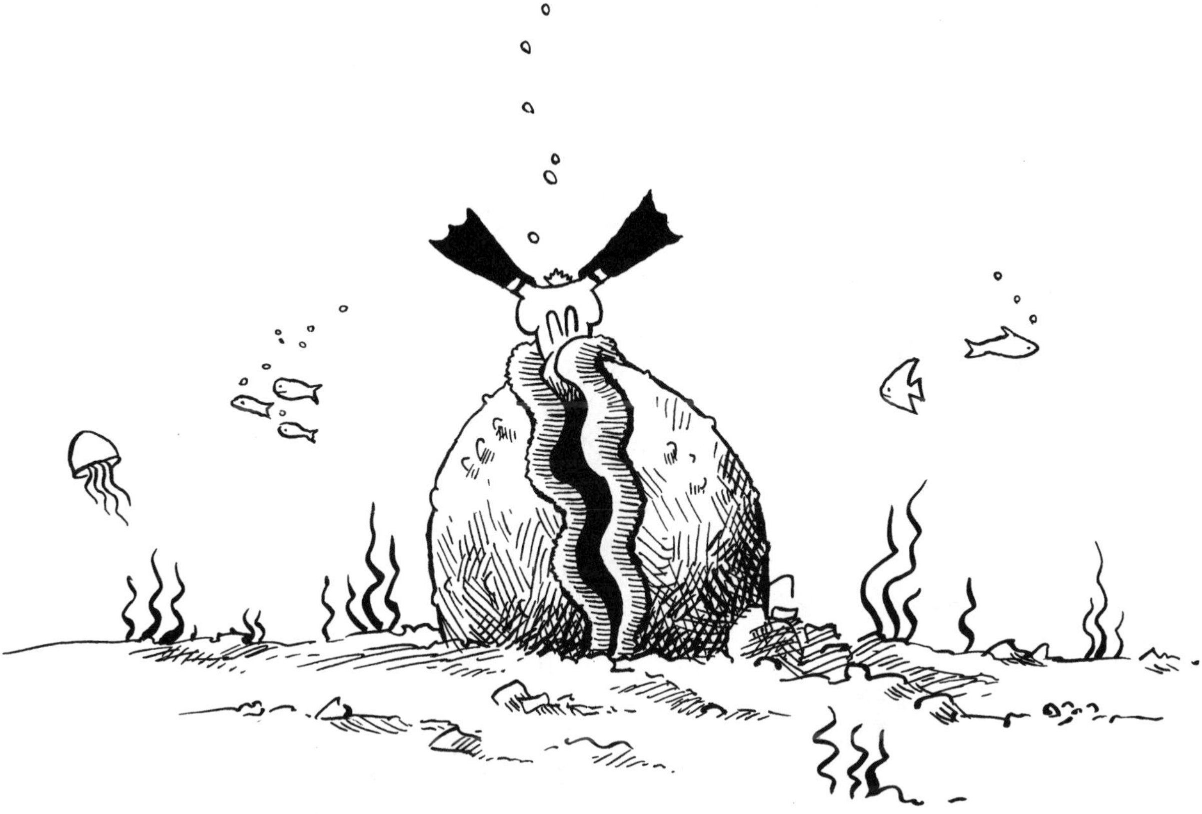

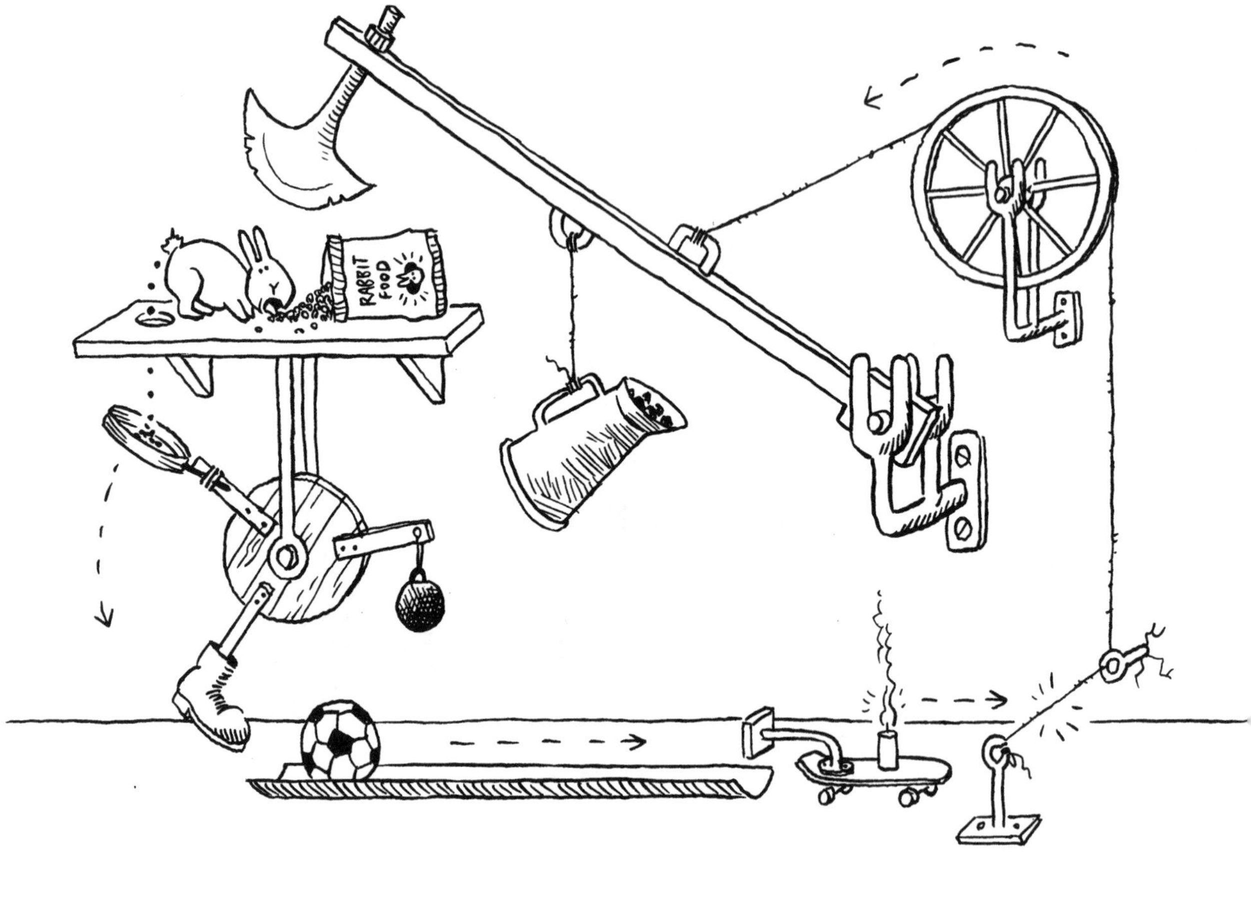
RABBIT FOOD

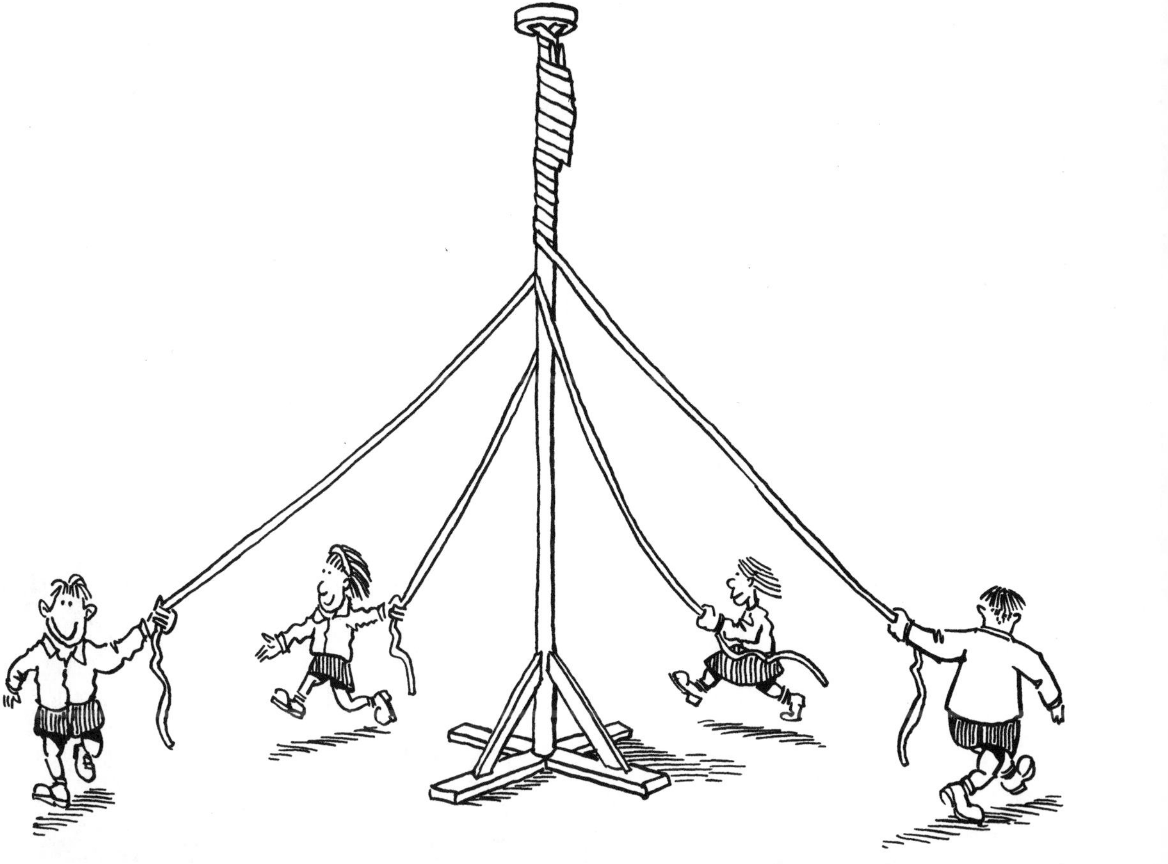

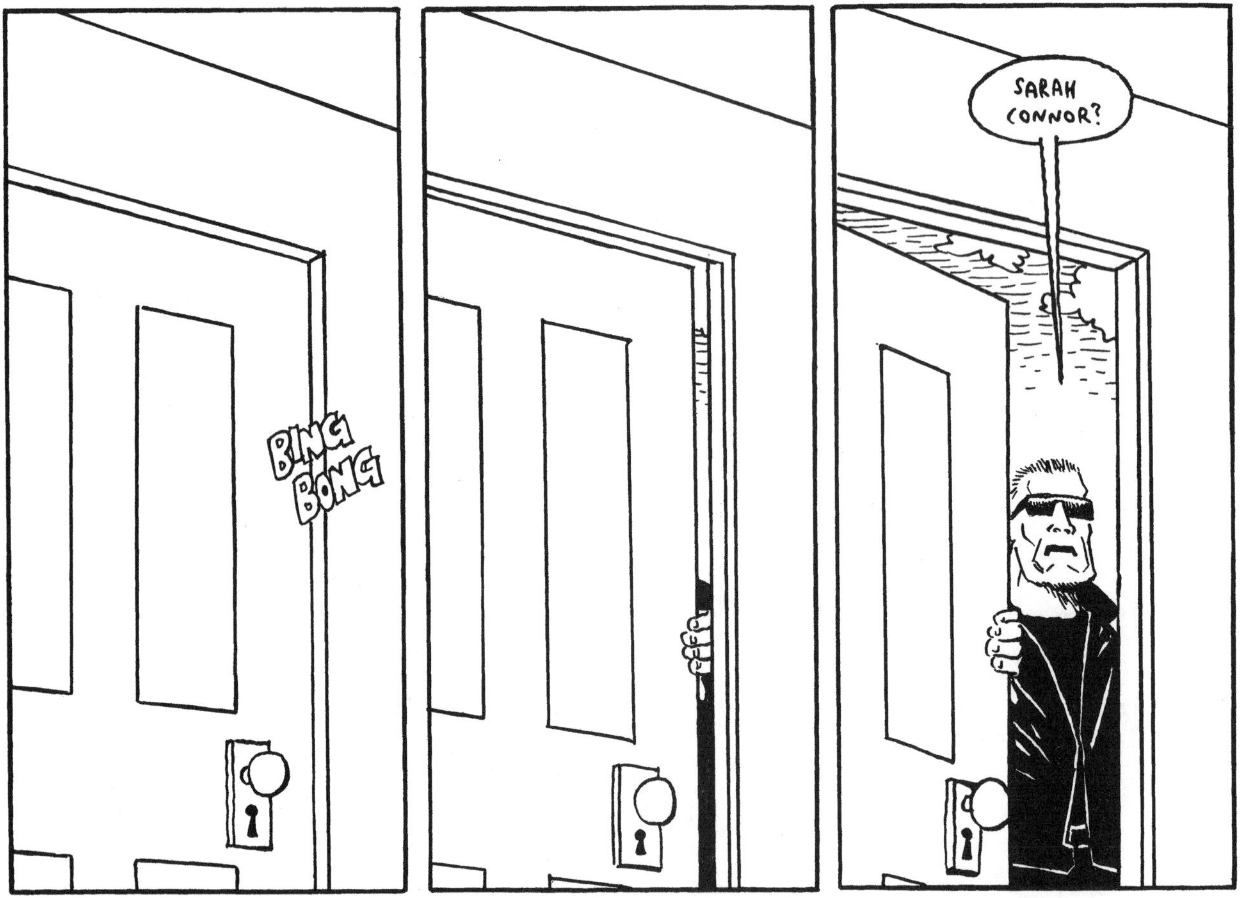
BING BONG
SARAH CONNOR?

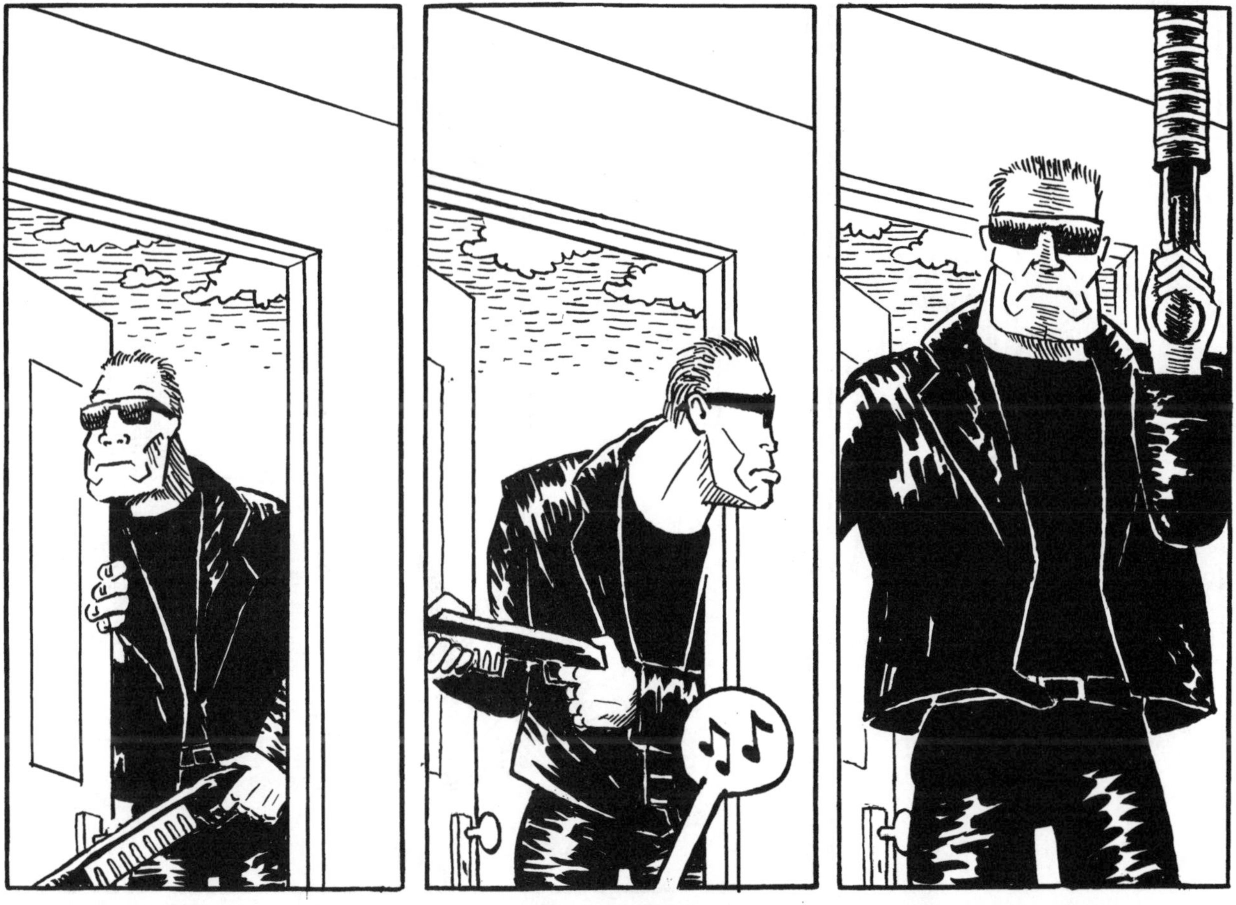

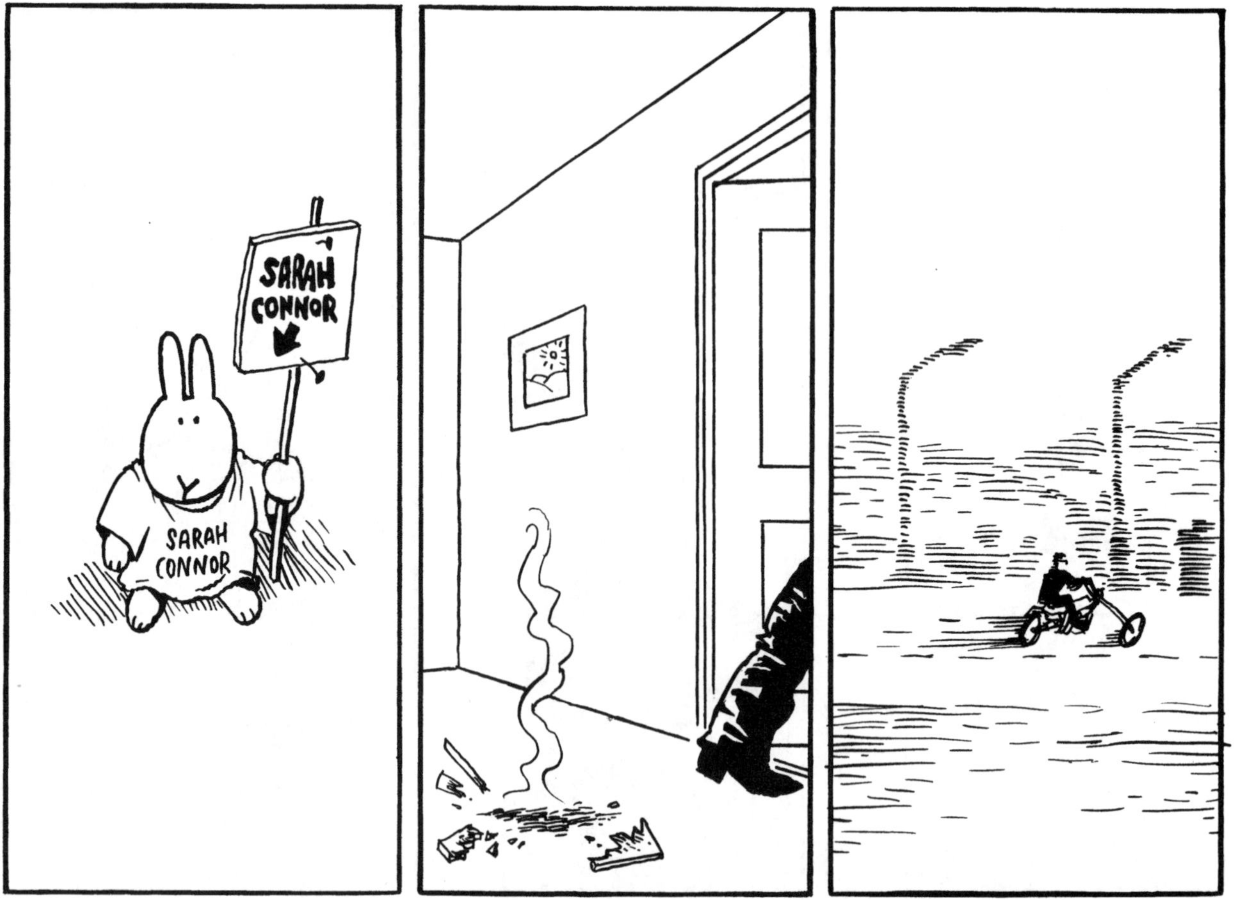
SARAH
CONNOR
SARAH
CONNOR

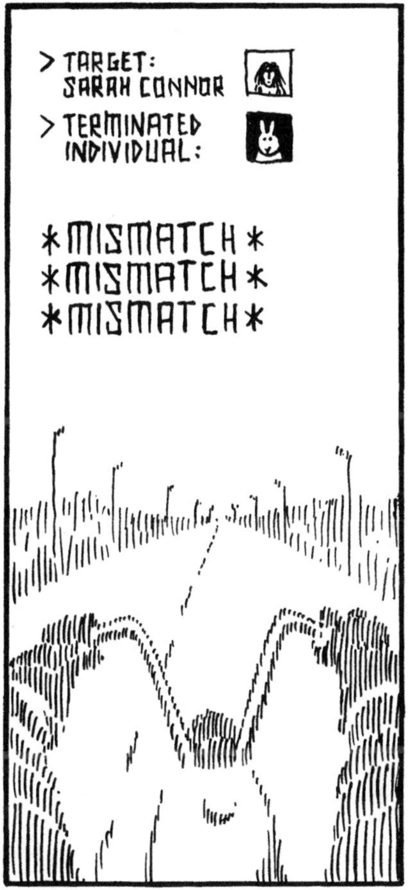
> TARGET:
SARAH CONNOR
> TERMINATED
INDIVIDUAL:
MISMATCH
MISMATCH
MISMATCH

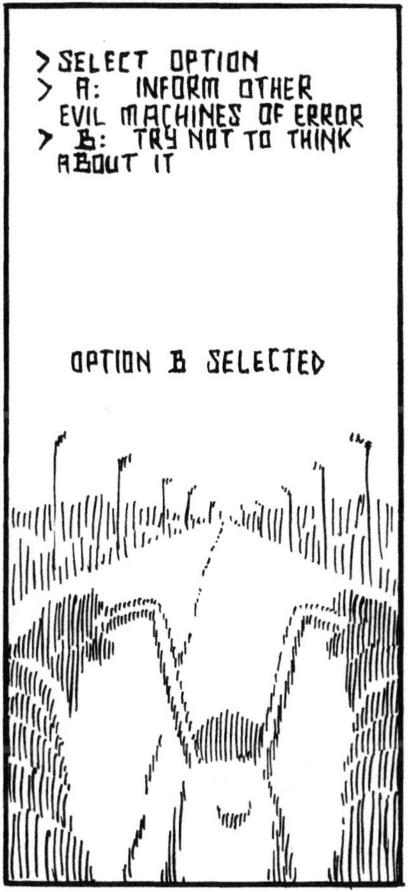
> SELECT OPTION
> A: INFORM OTHER
EVIL MACHINES OF ERROR
> B: TRY NOT TO THINK
ABOUT IT
OPTION B SELECTED

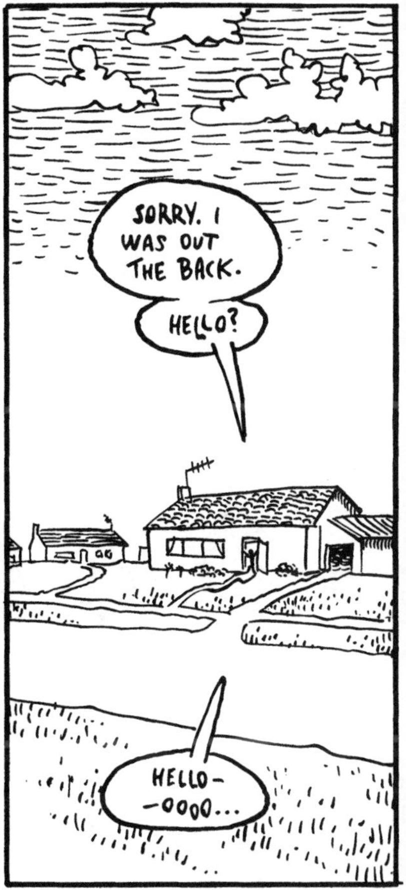
HELLO-
-OOOO...
HELLO?
SORRY. I
WAS OUT
THE BACK.

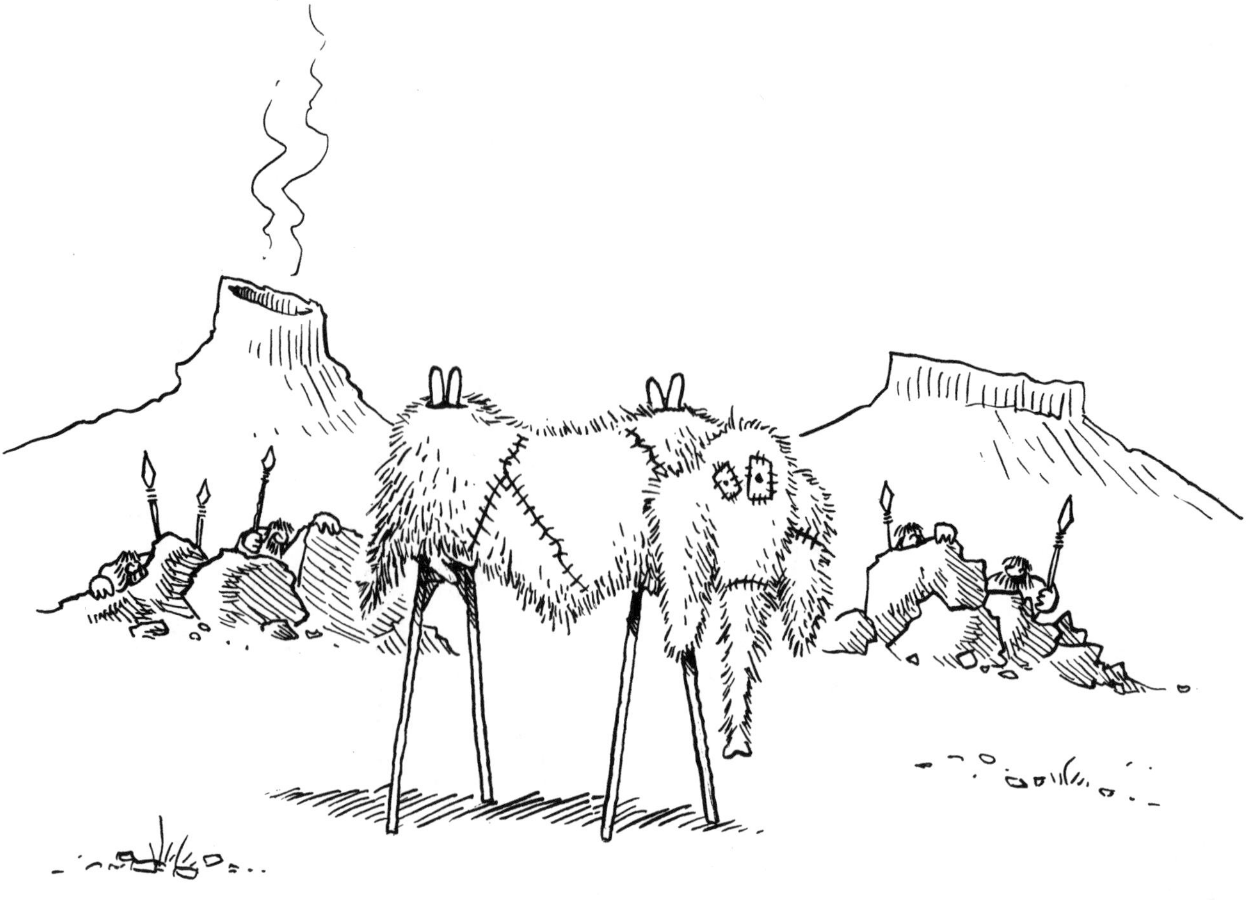

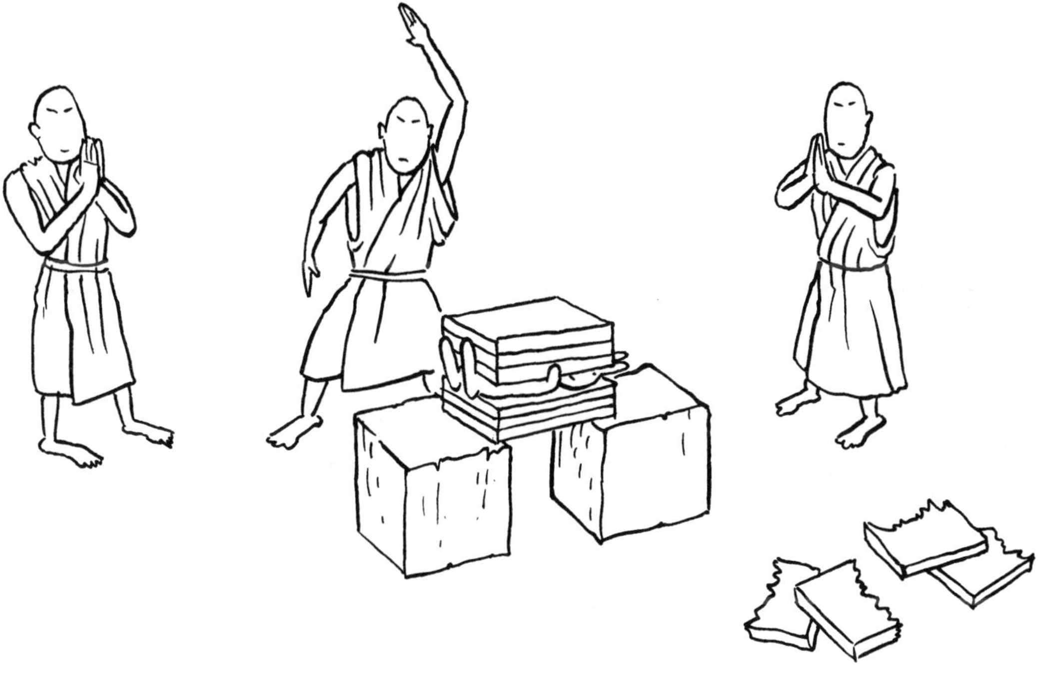

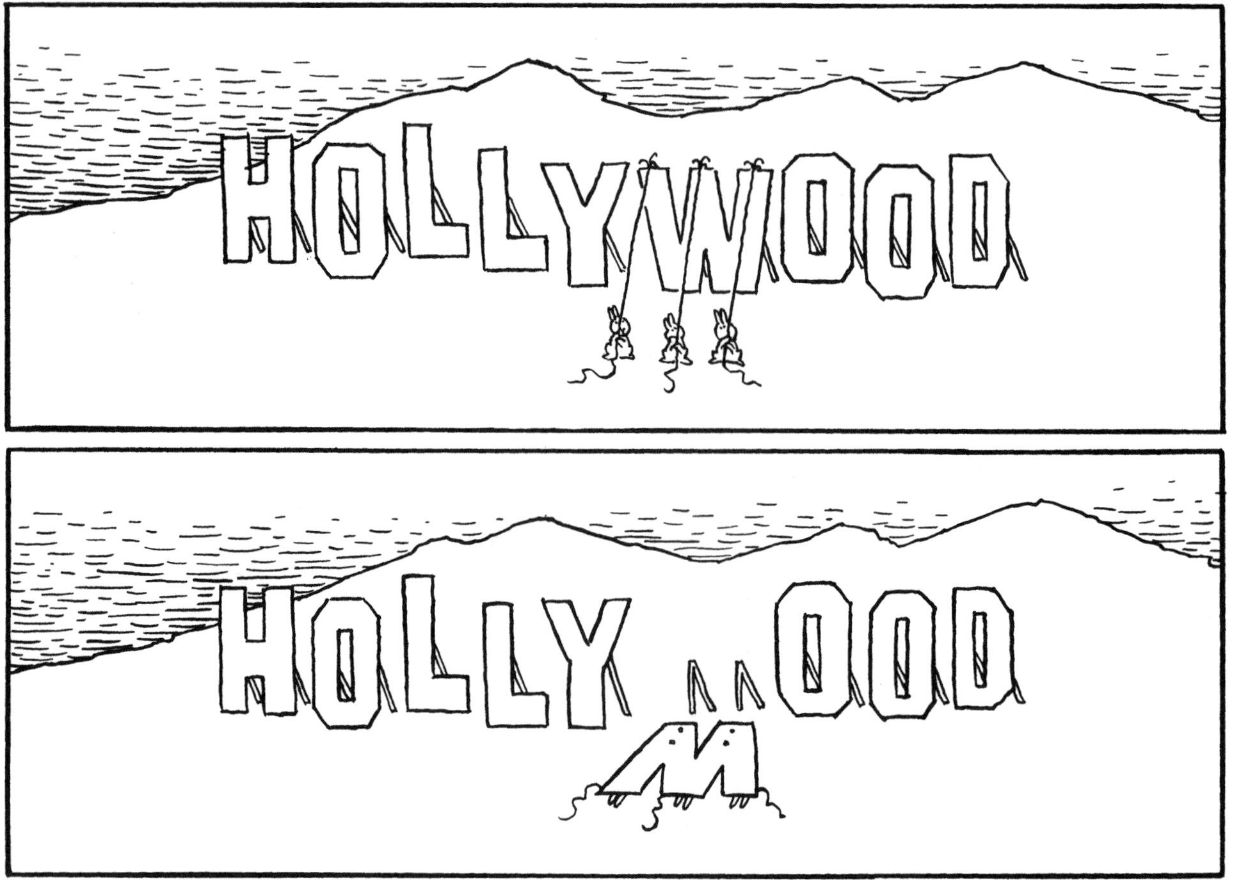
HOLLYWOOD
HOLLY OOD

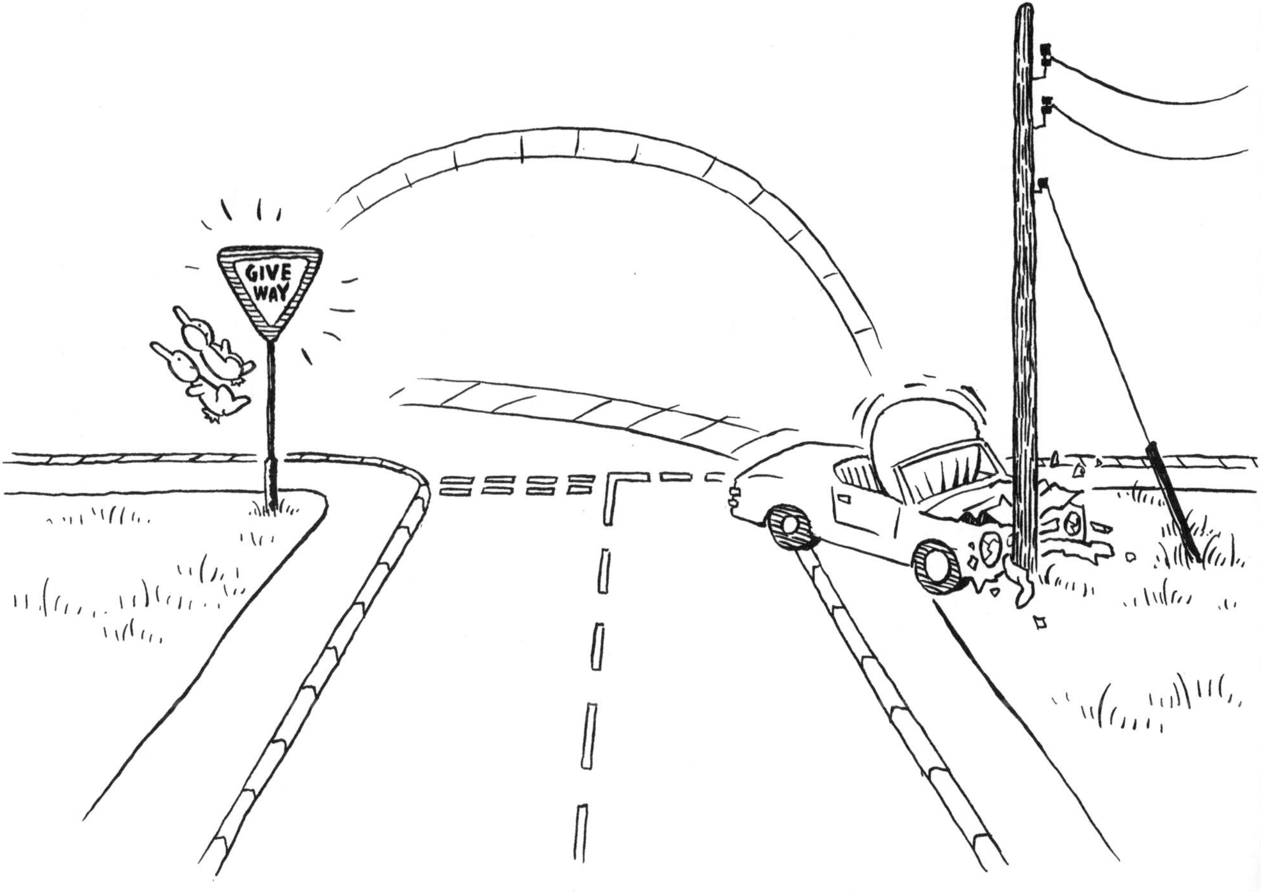
GIVE WAY

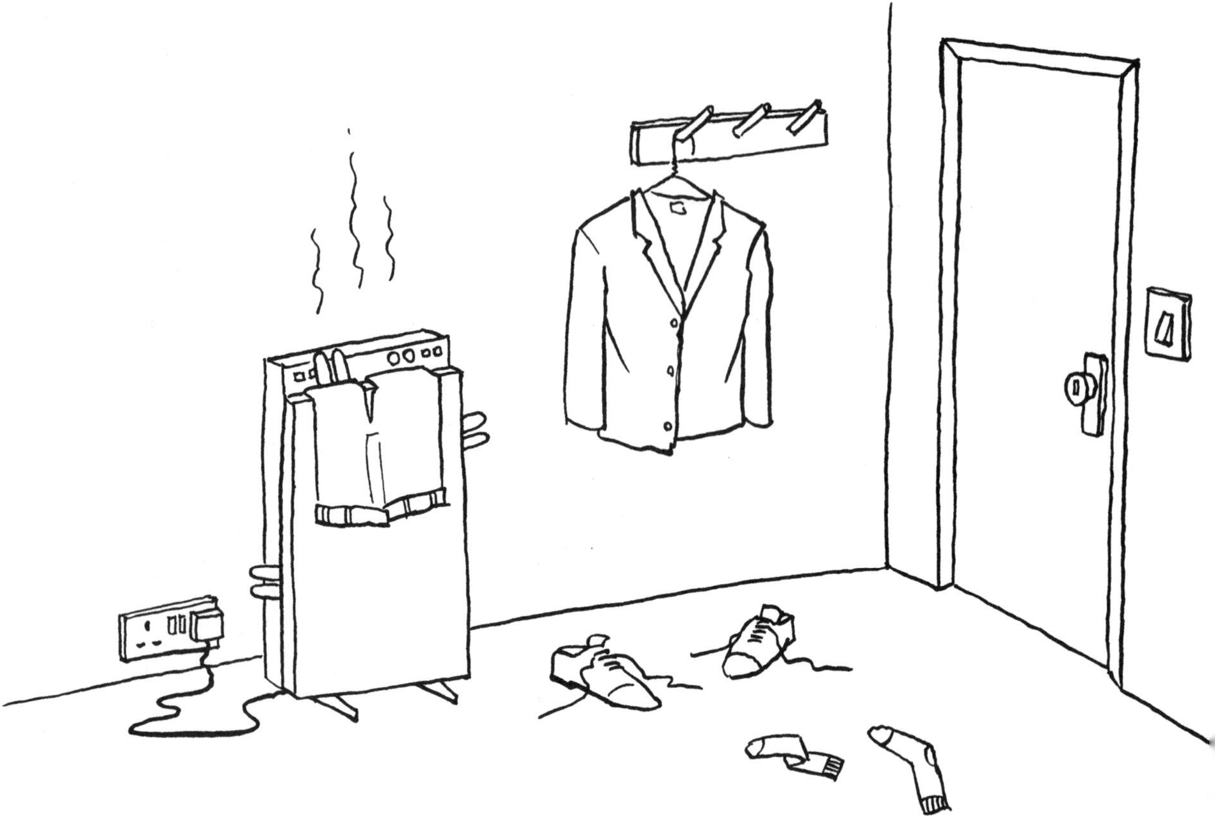

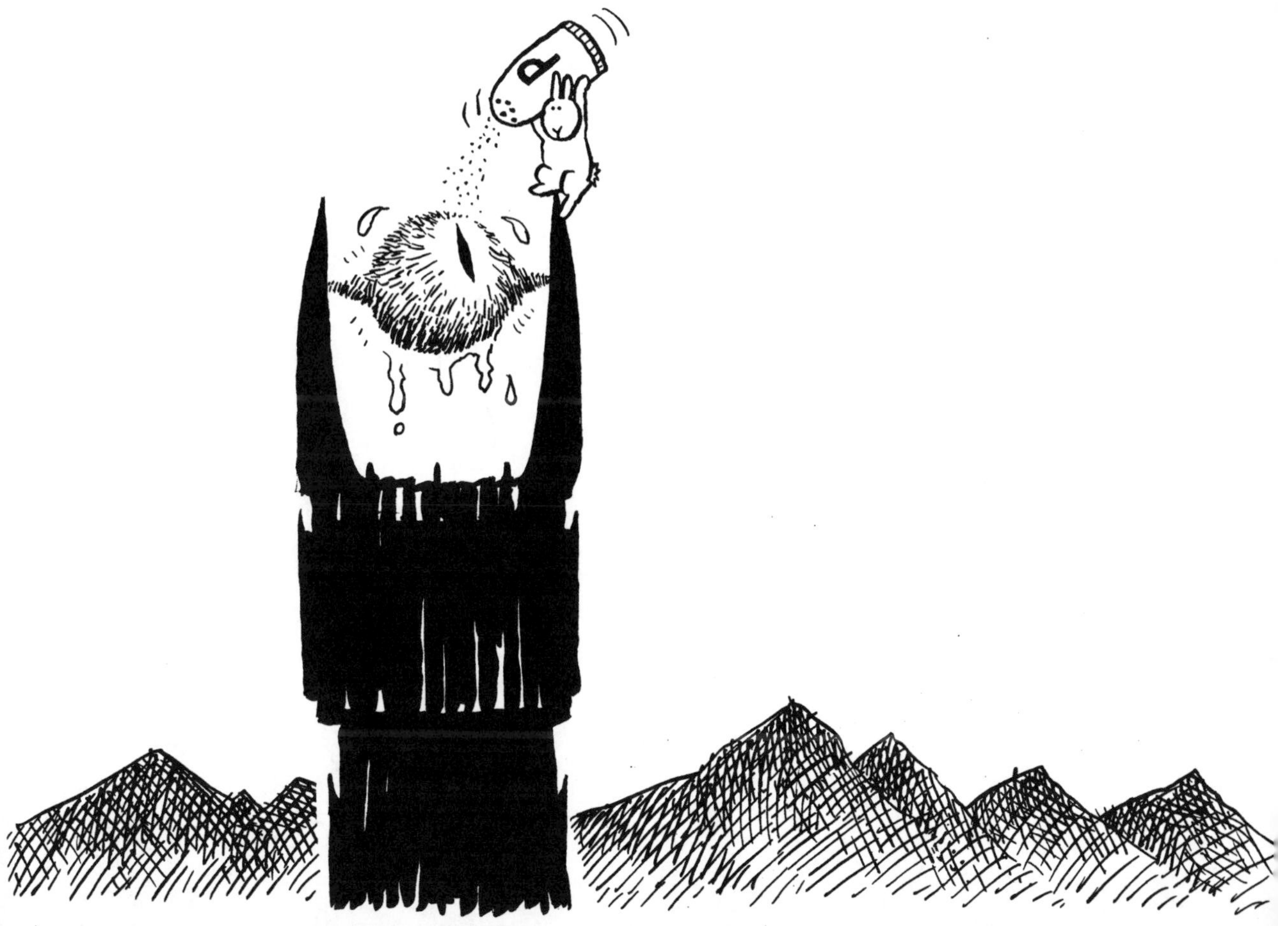
P

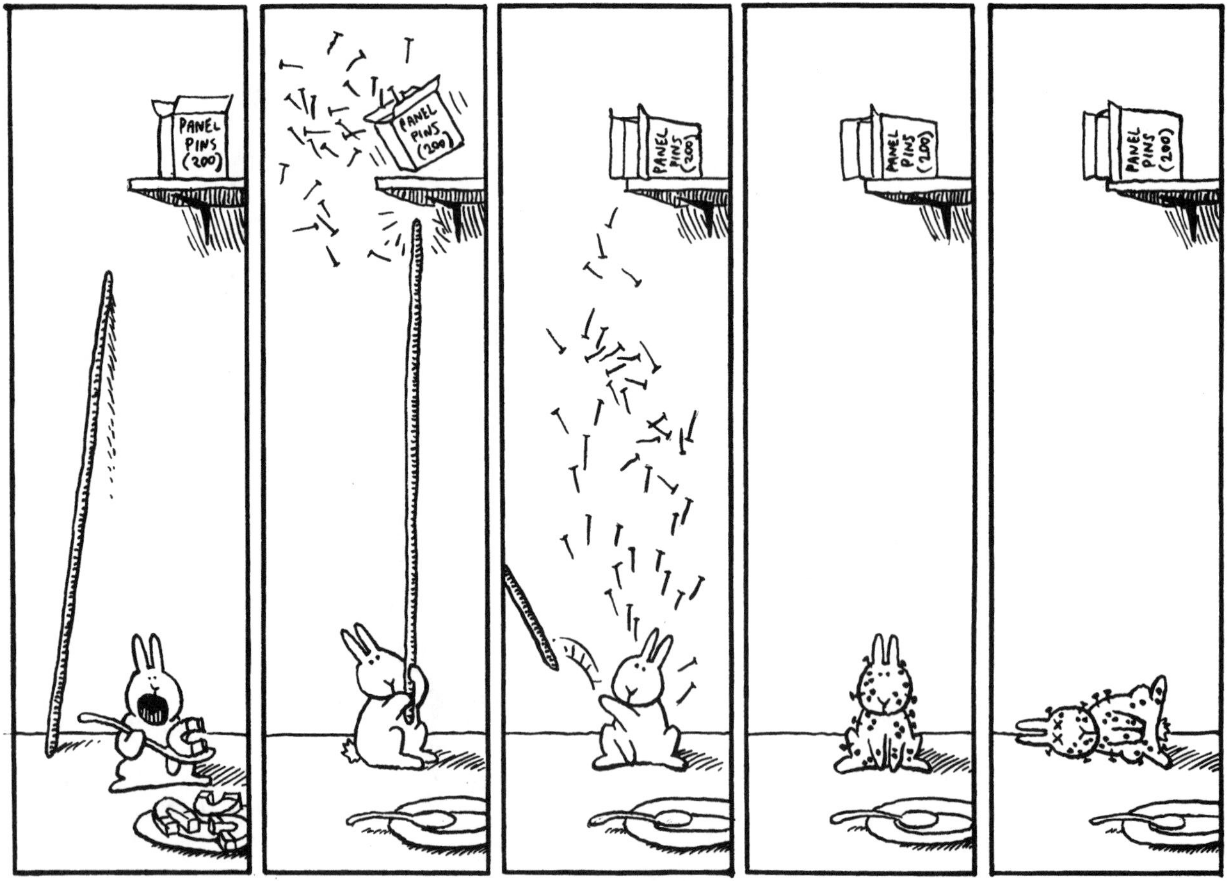
PANEL PINS (200)

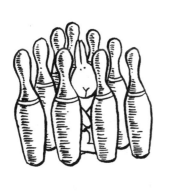
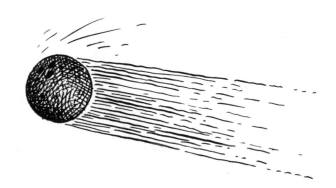

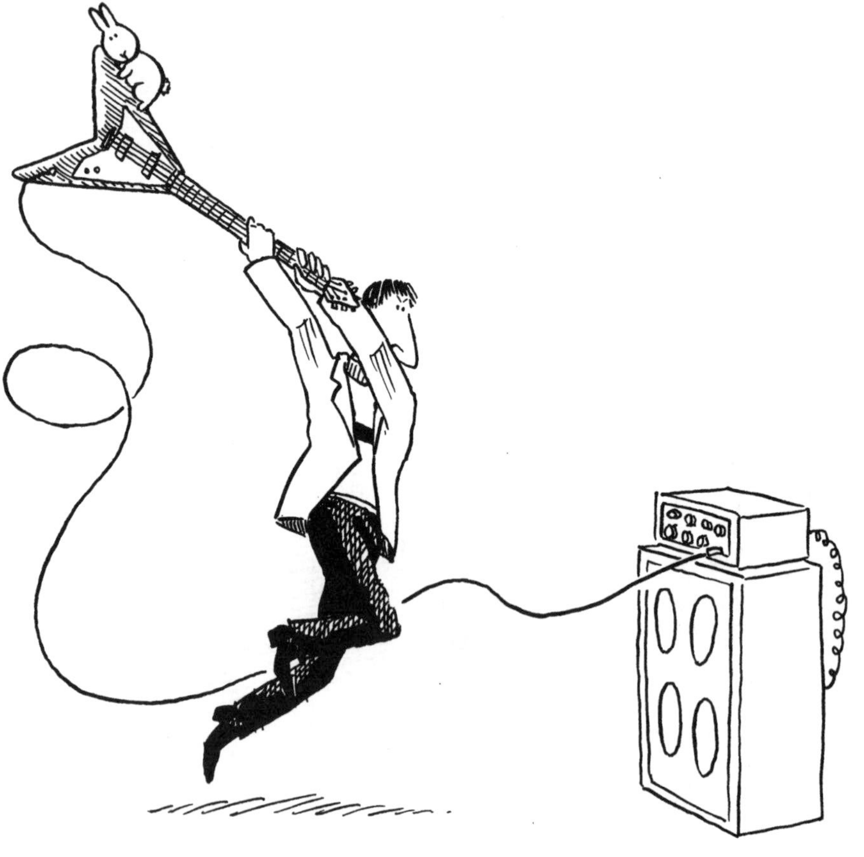

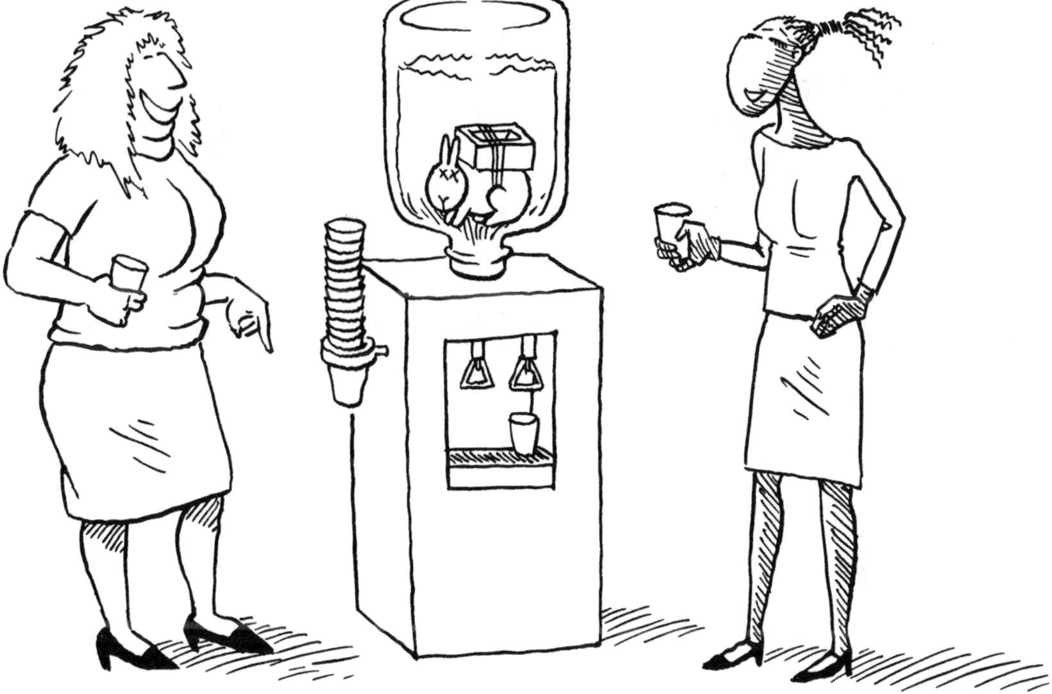

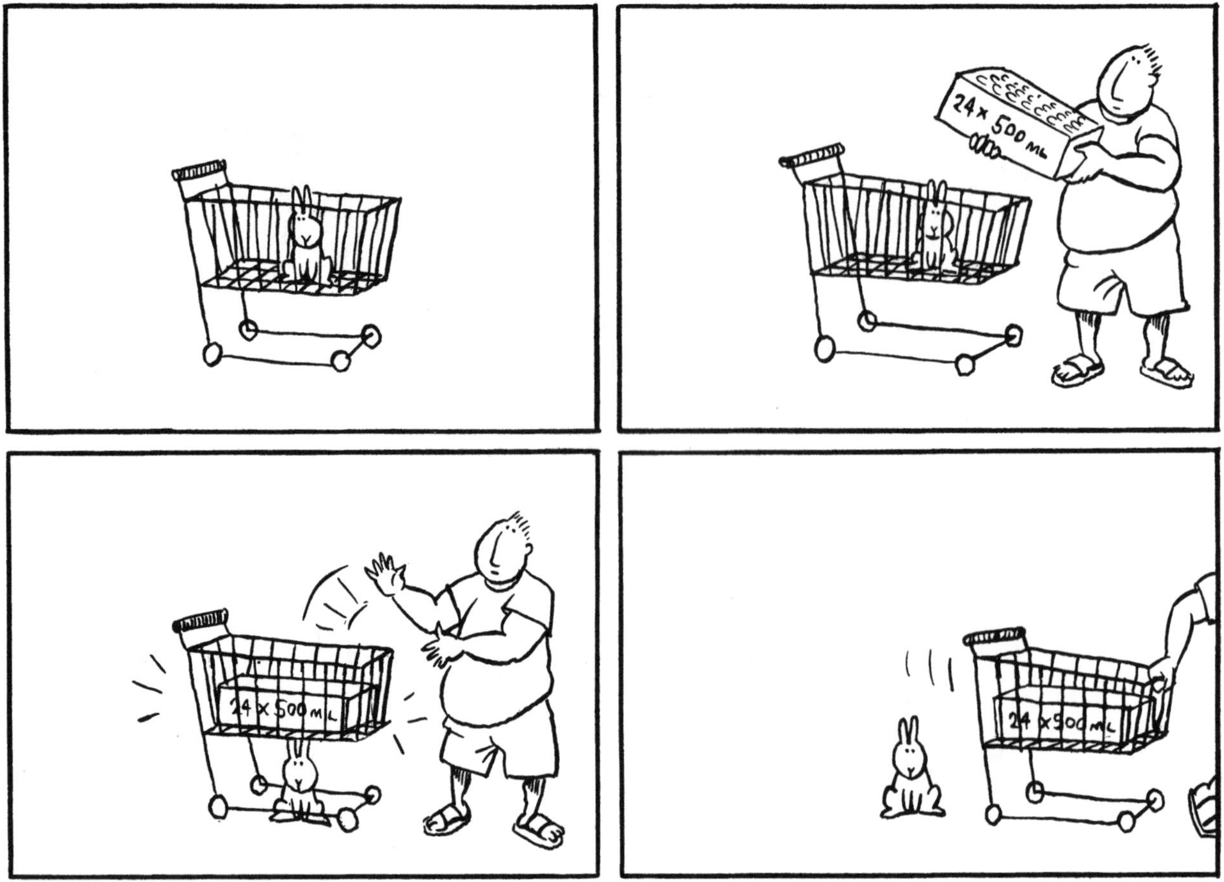
24 x 500 mL
24 x 500 mL
24 x 500 mL

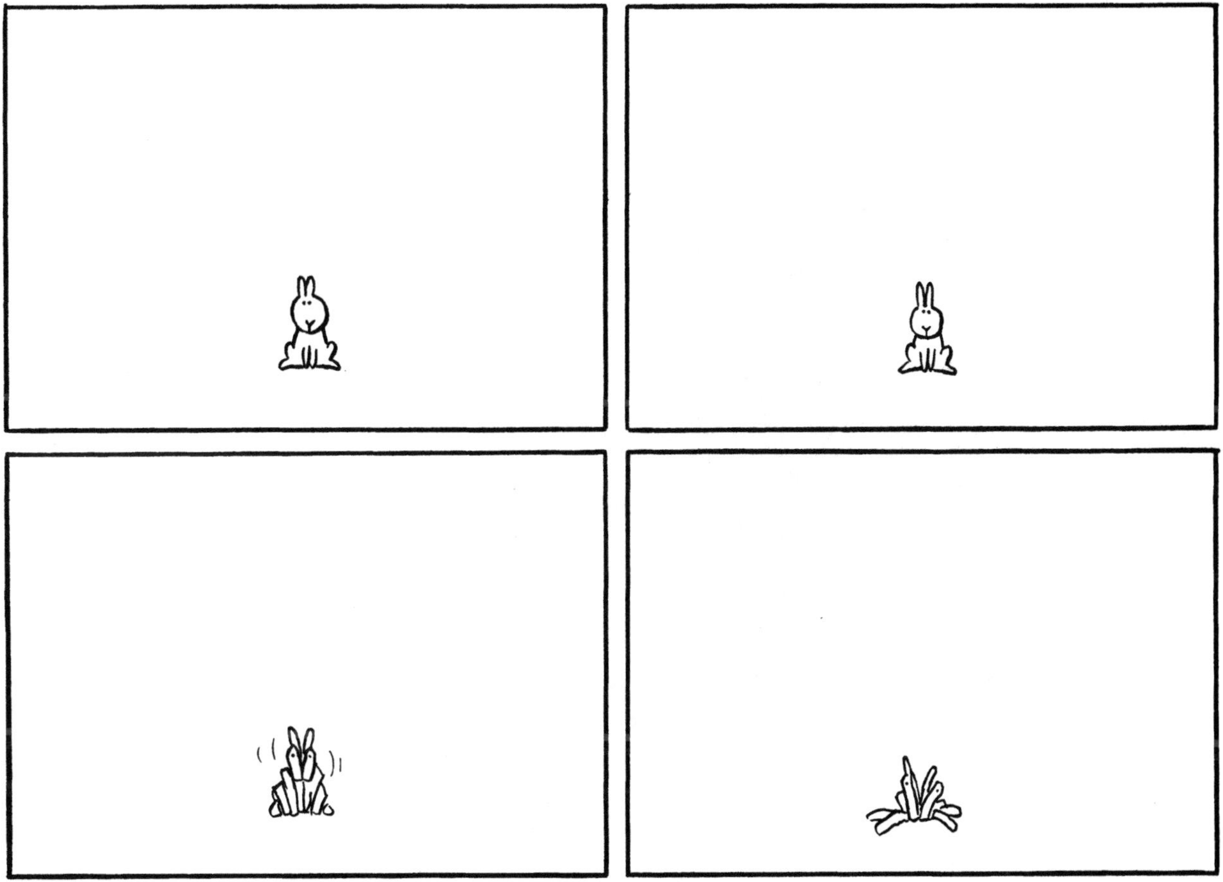

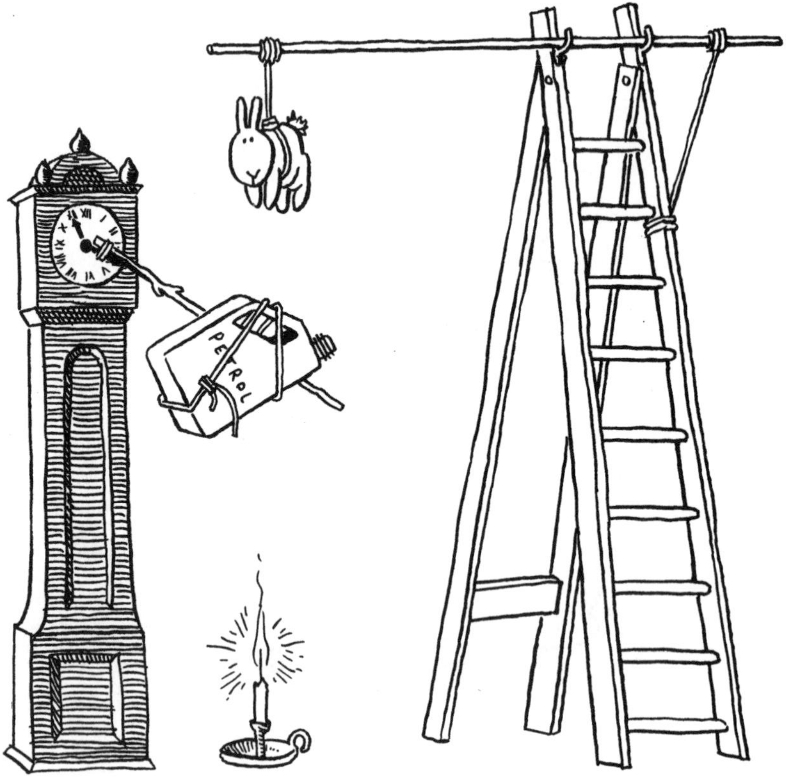
PETROL

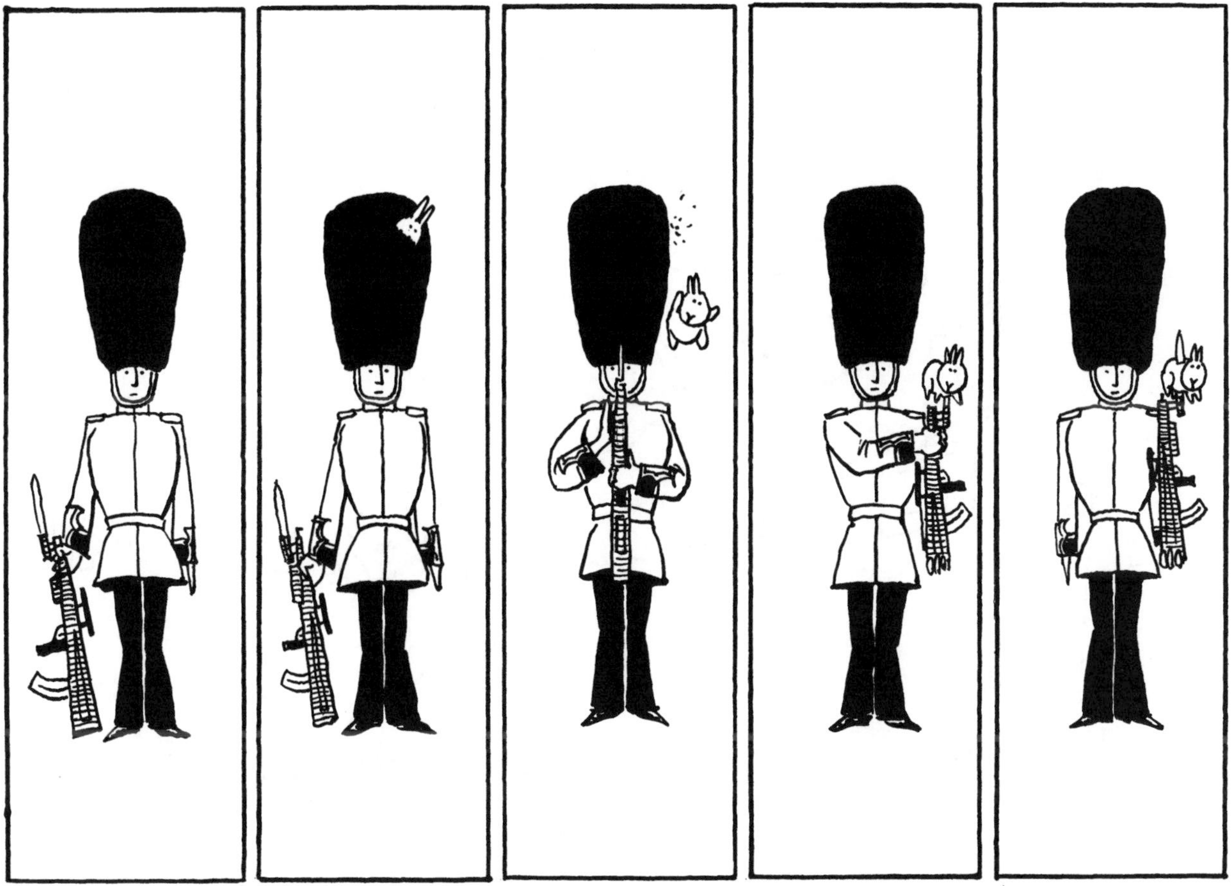

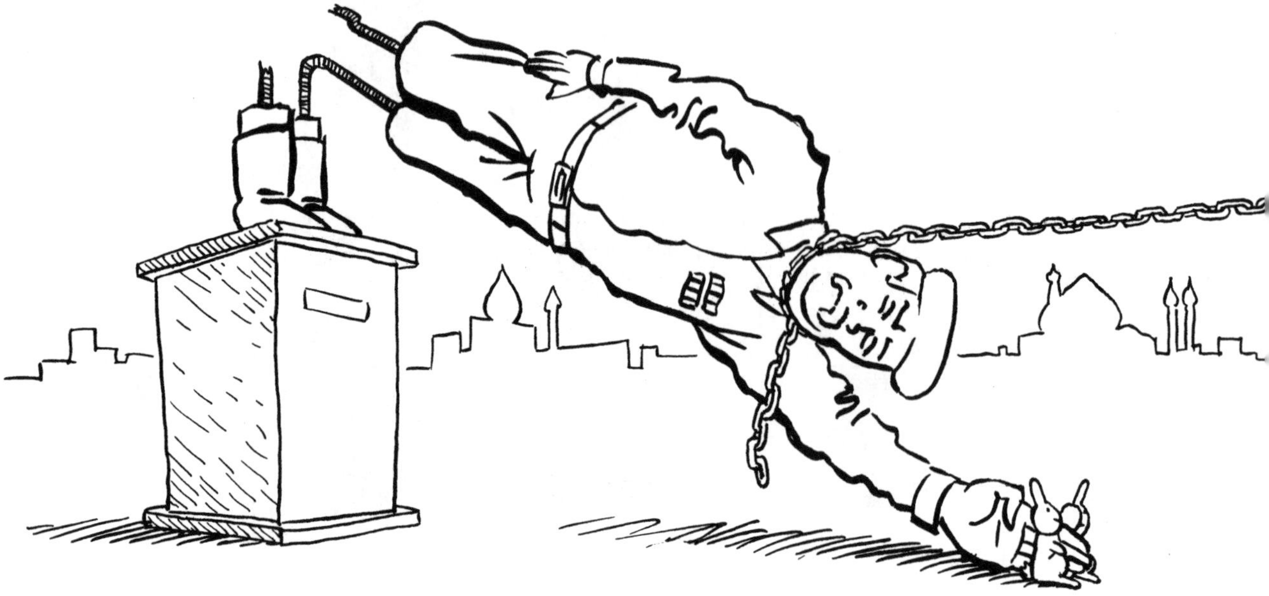

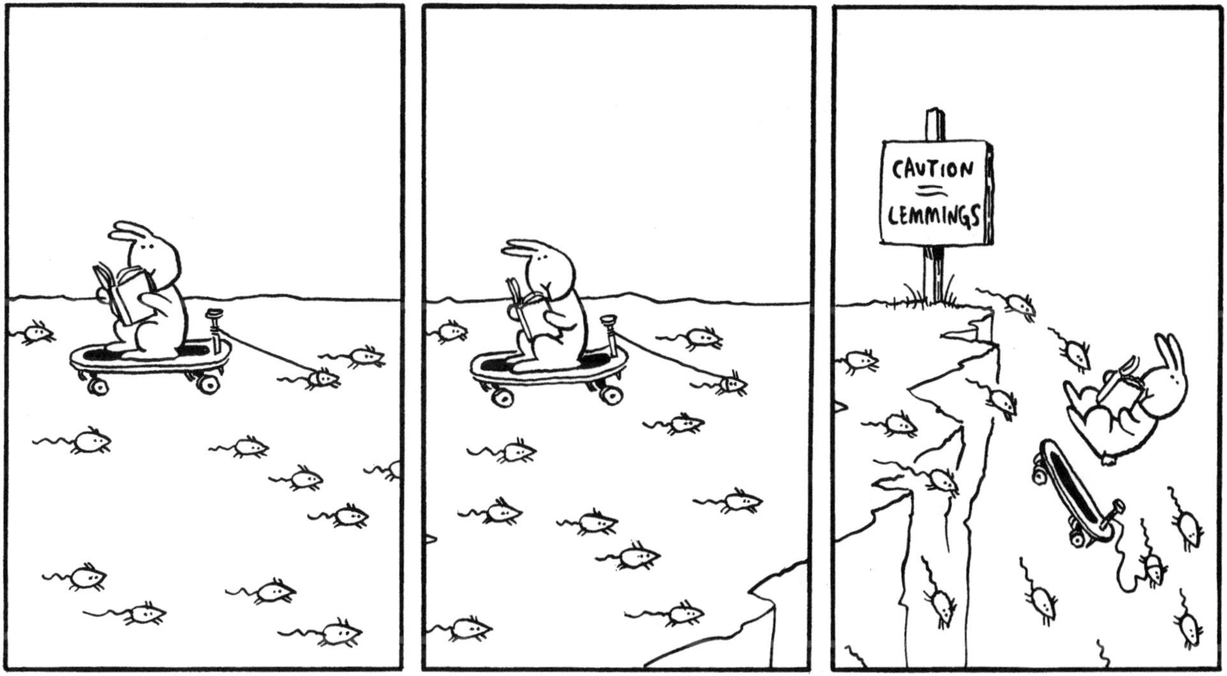
CAUTION
=
LEMMINGS

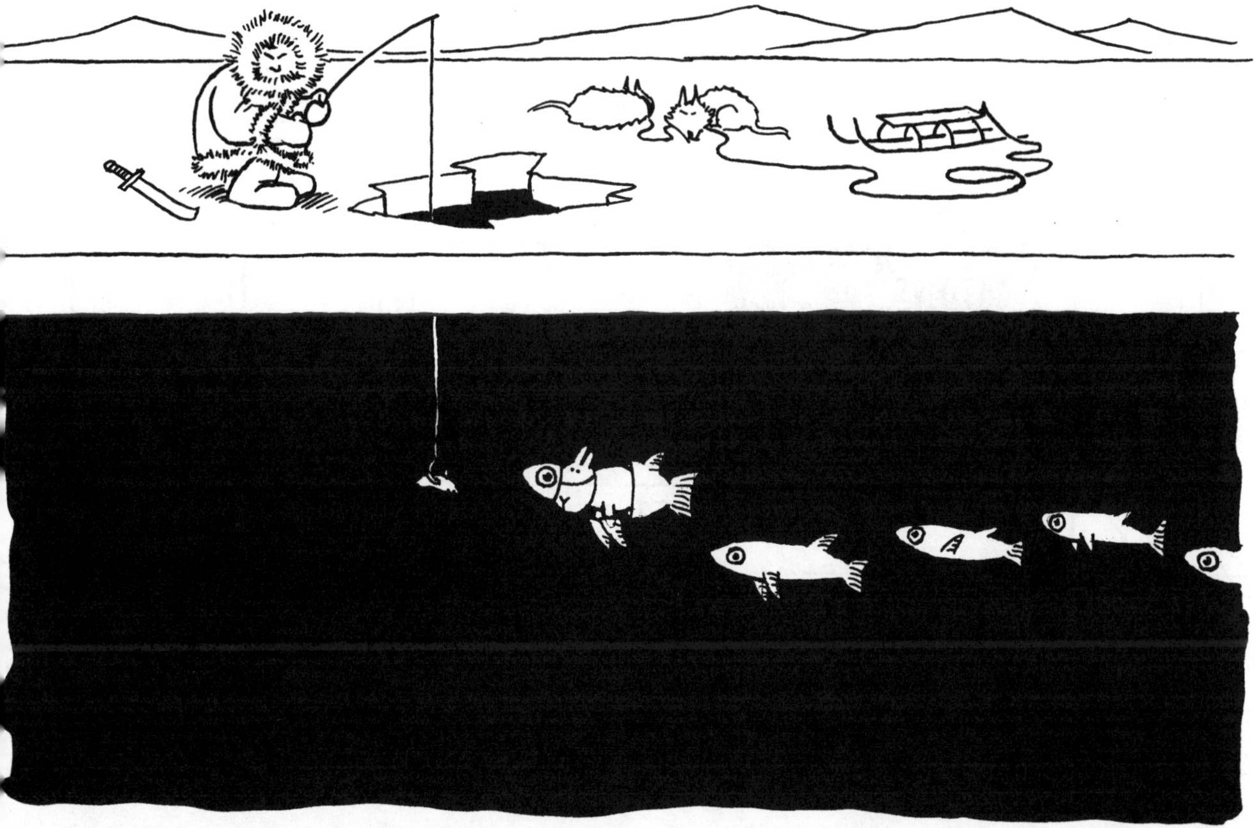

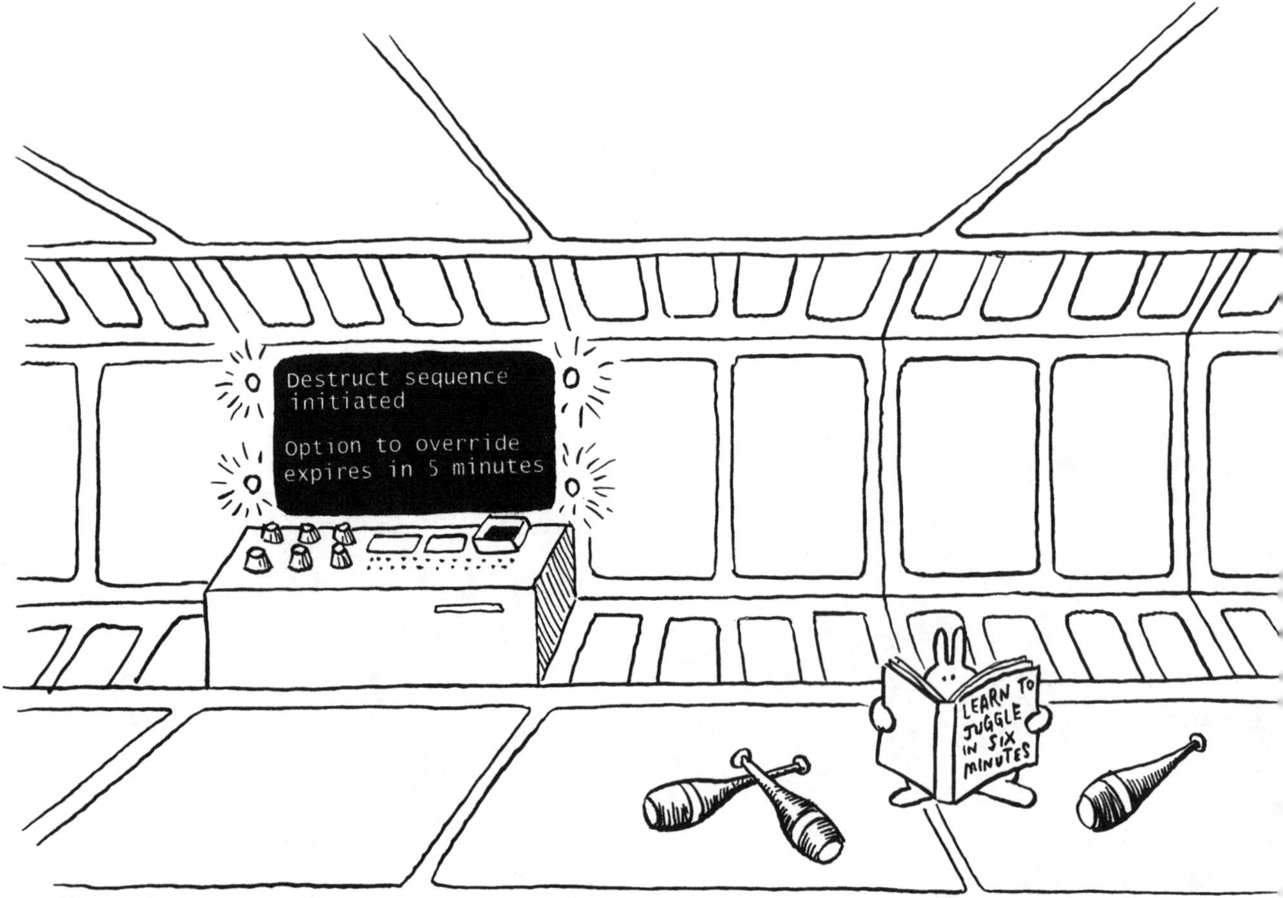
Destruct sequence
initiated
Option to override
expires in 5 minutes
LEARN TO
JUGGLE
IN SIX
MINUTES

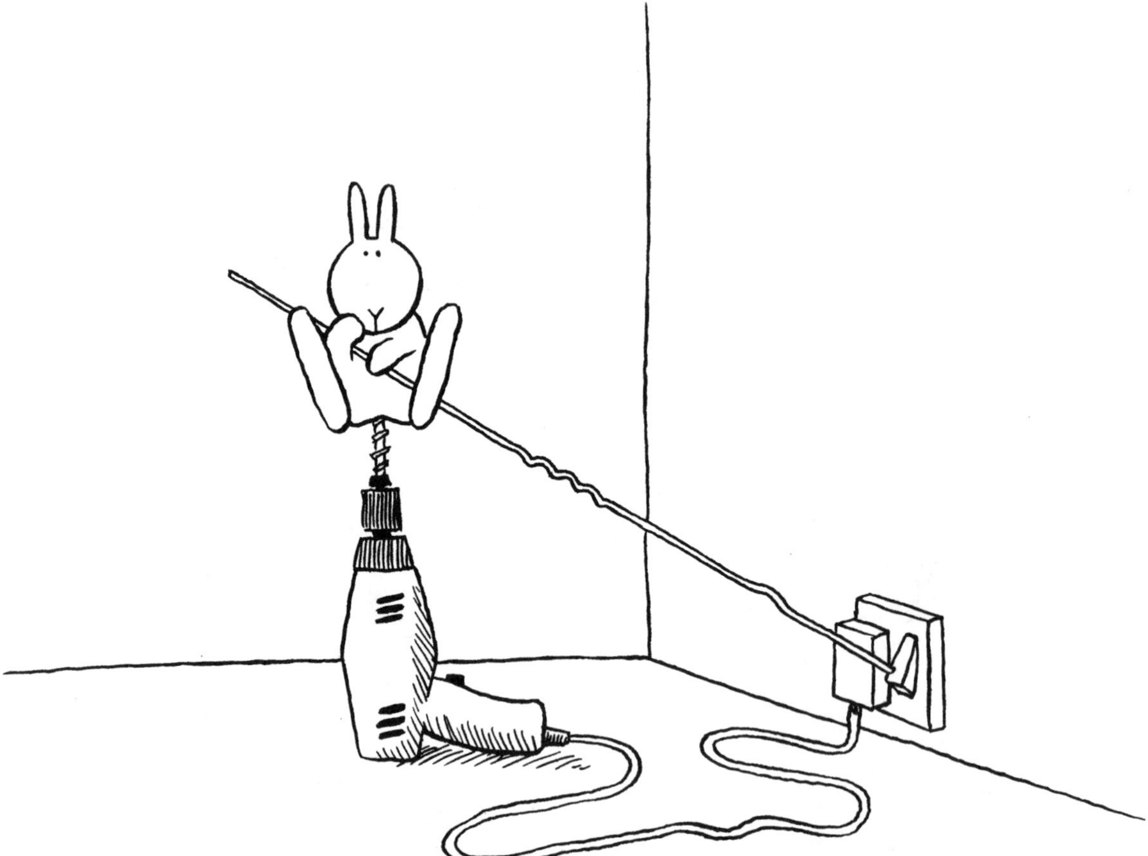

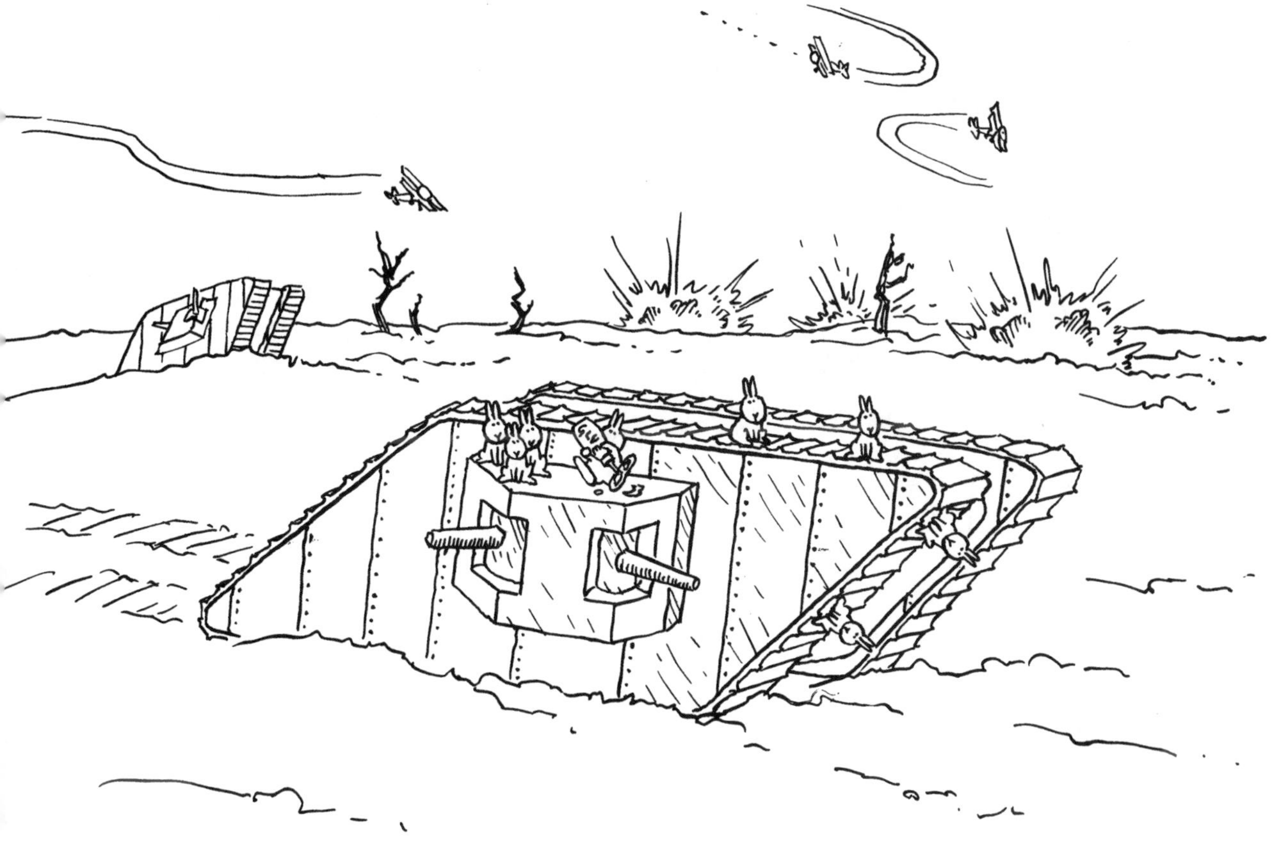
GLU

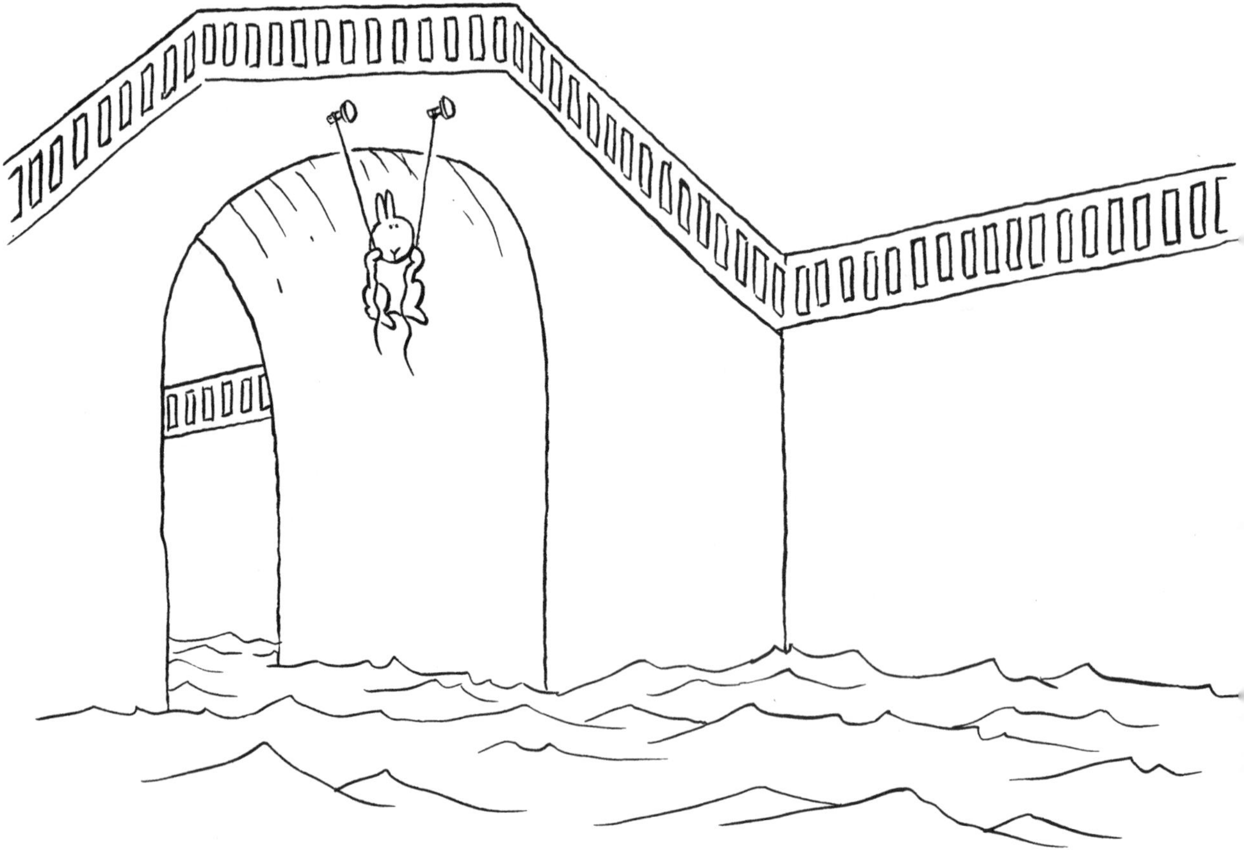

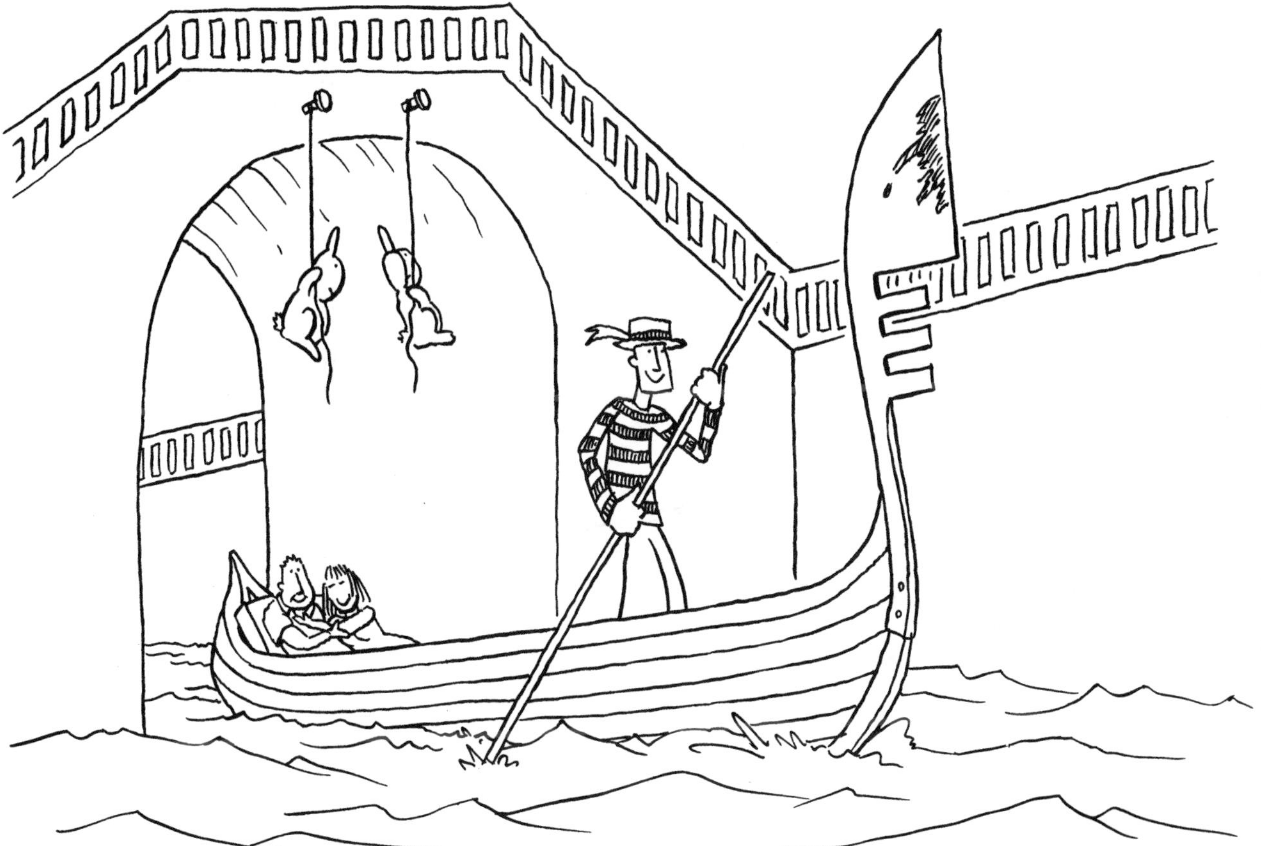

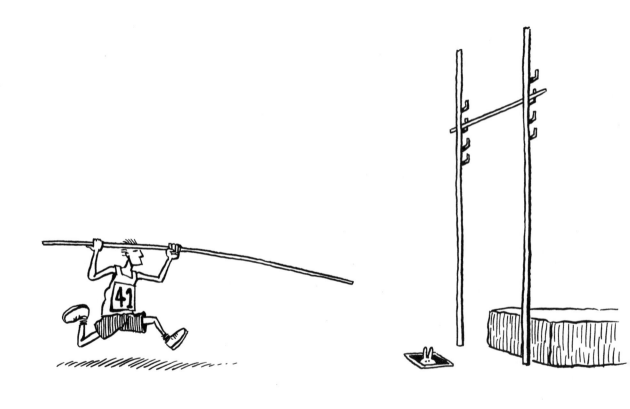

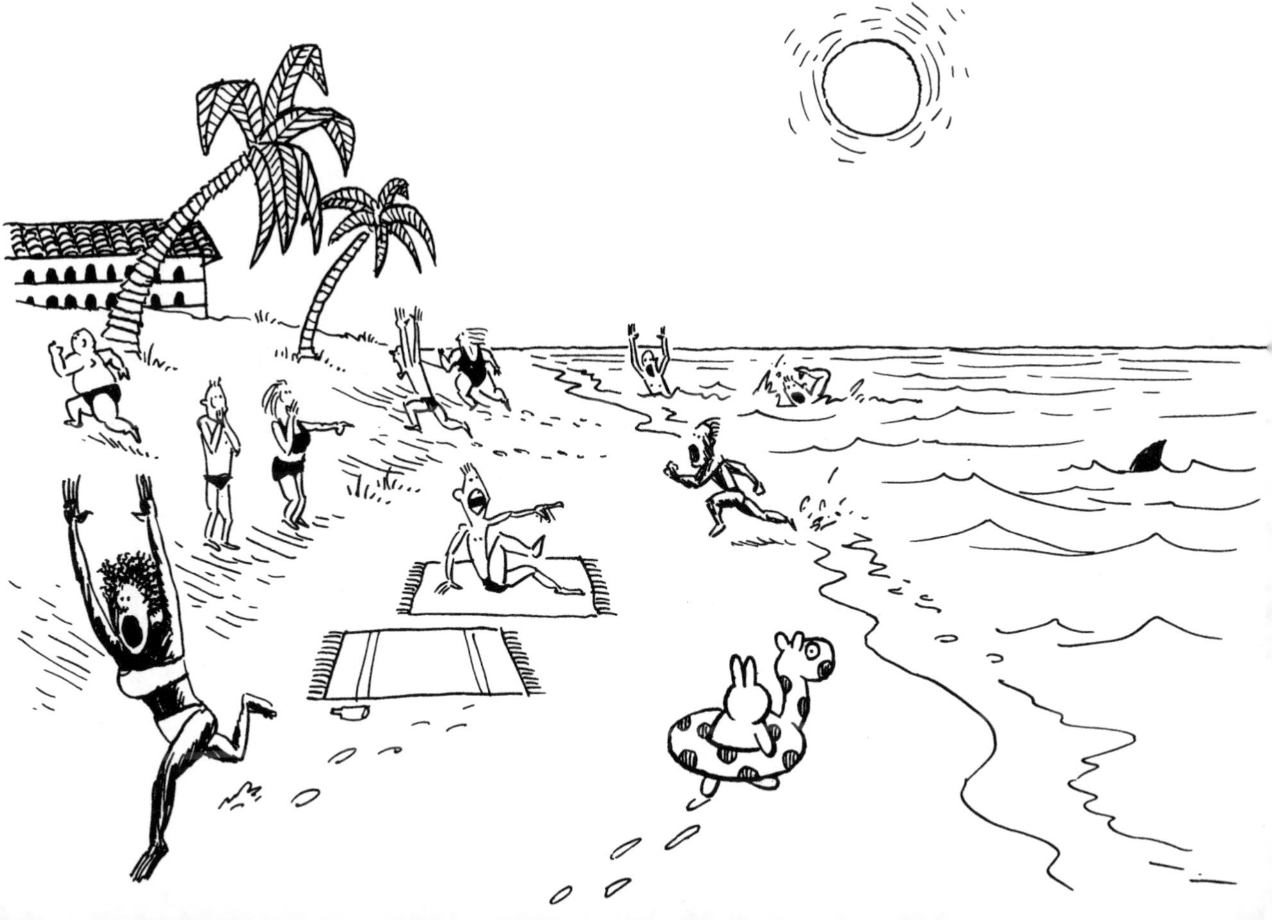

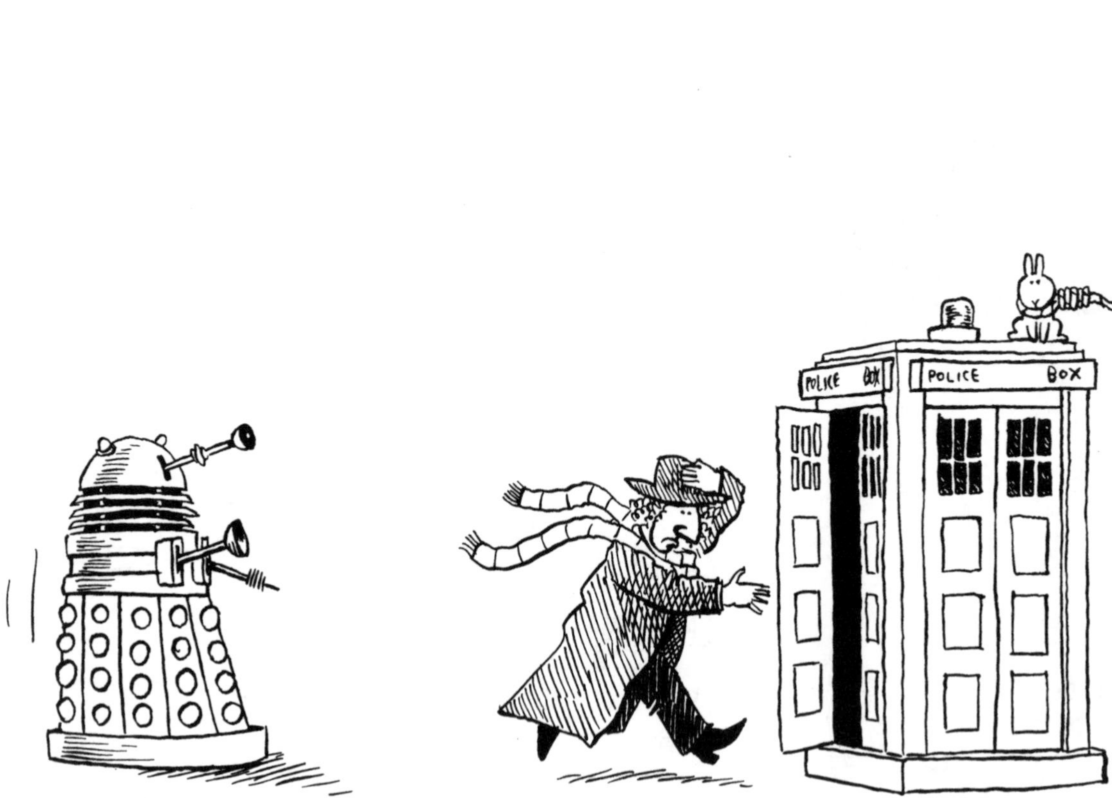
POLICE BOX
POLICE BOX

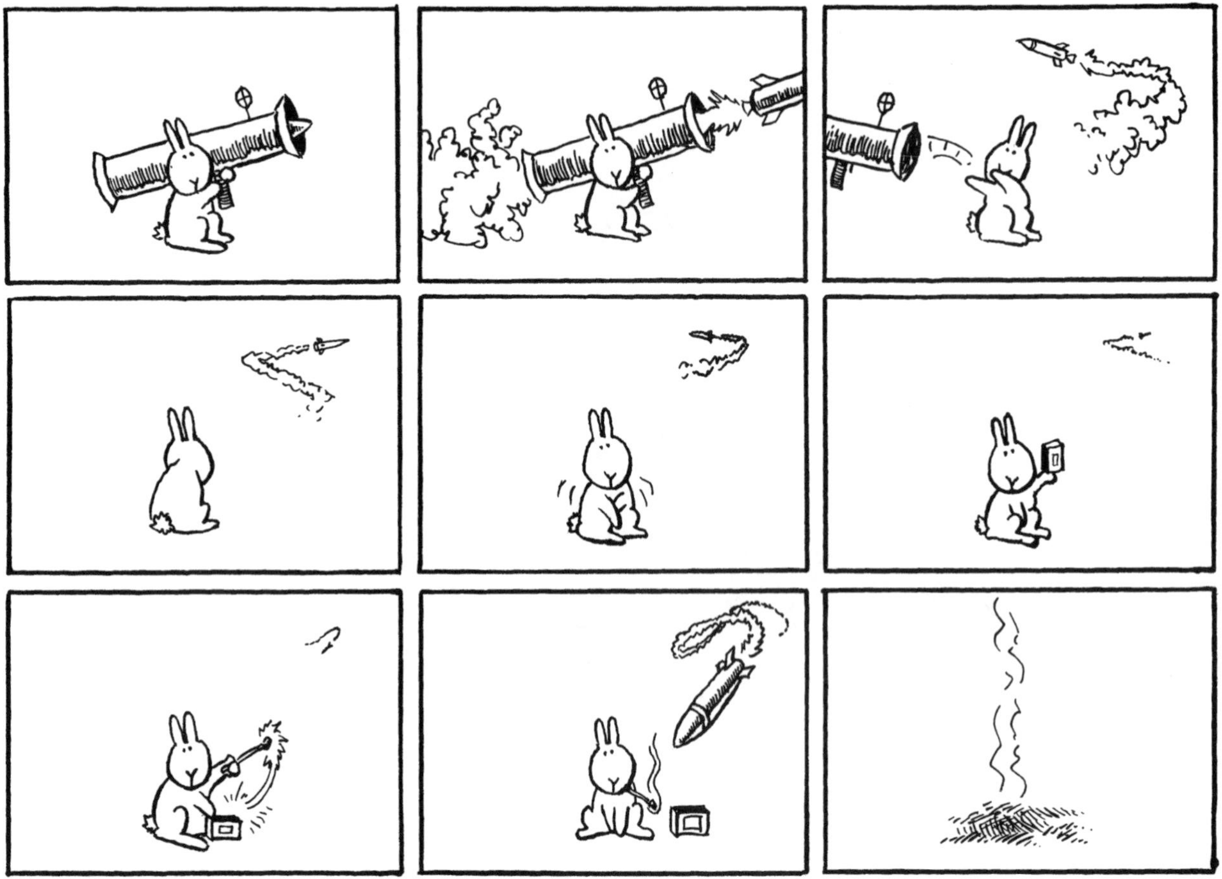

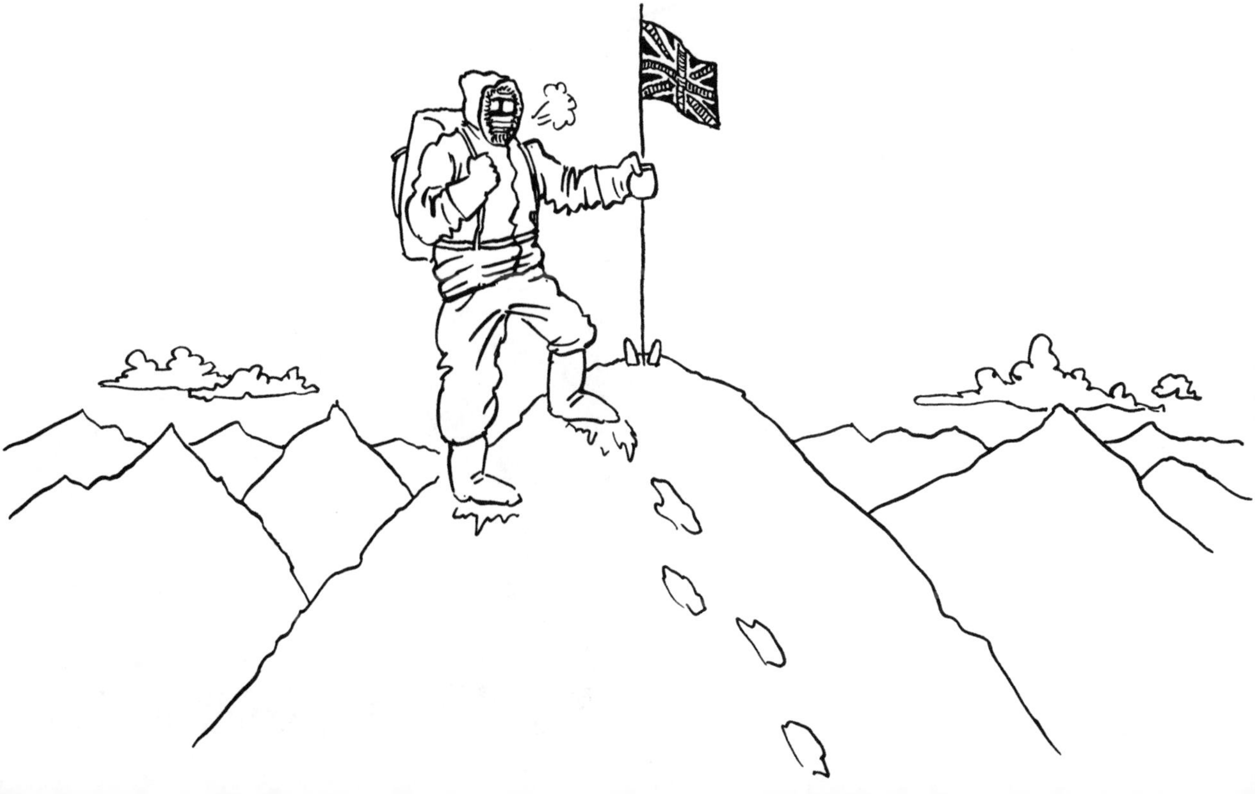

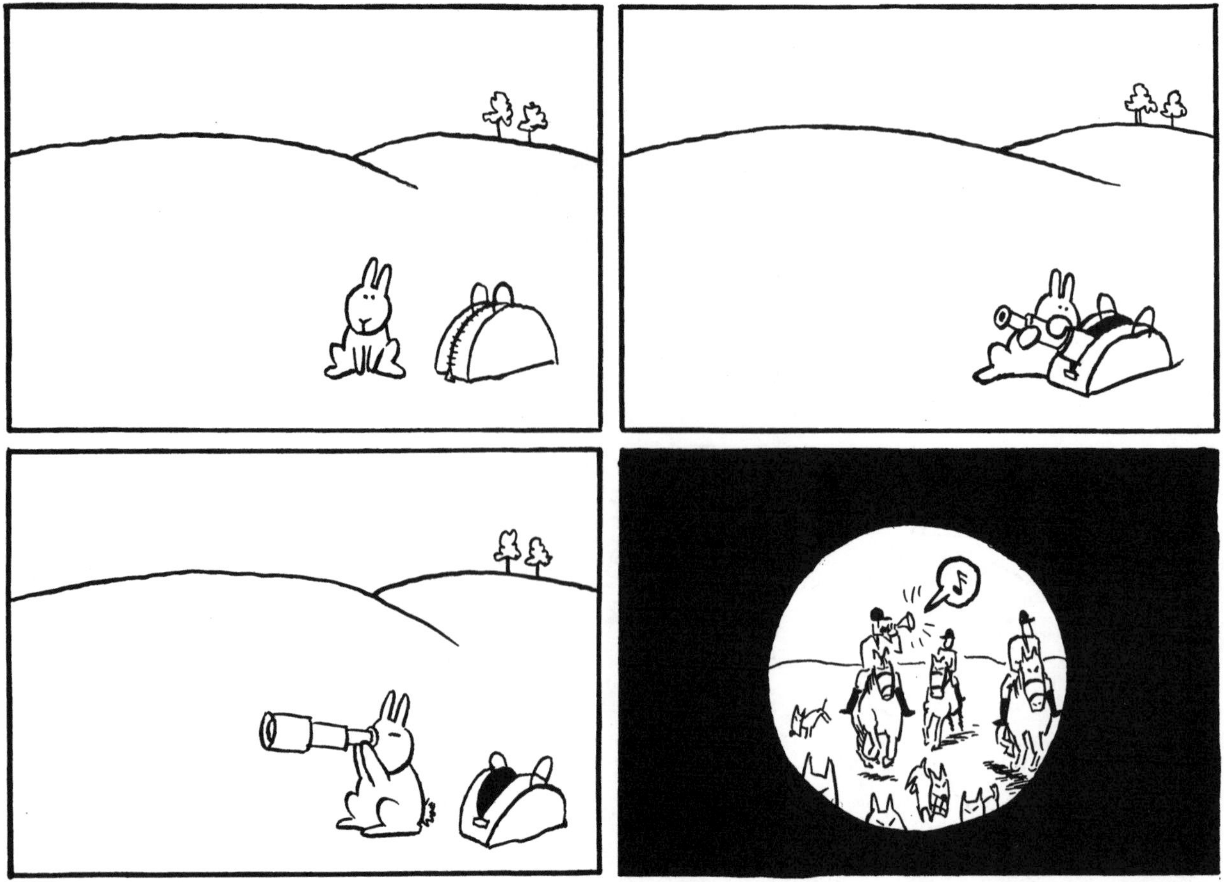

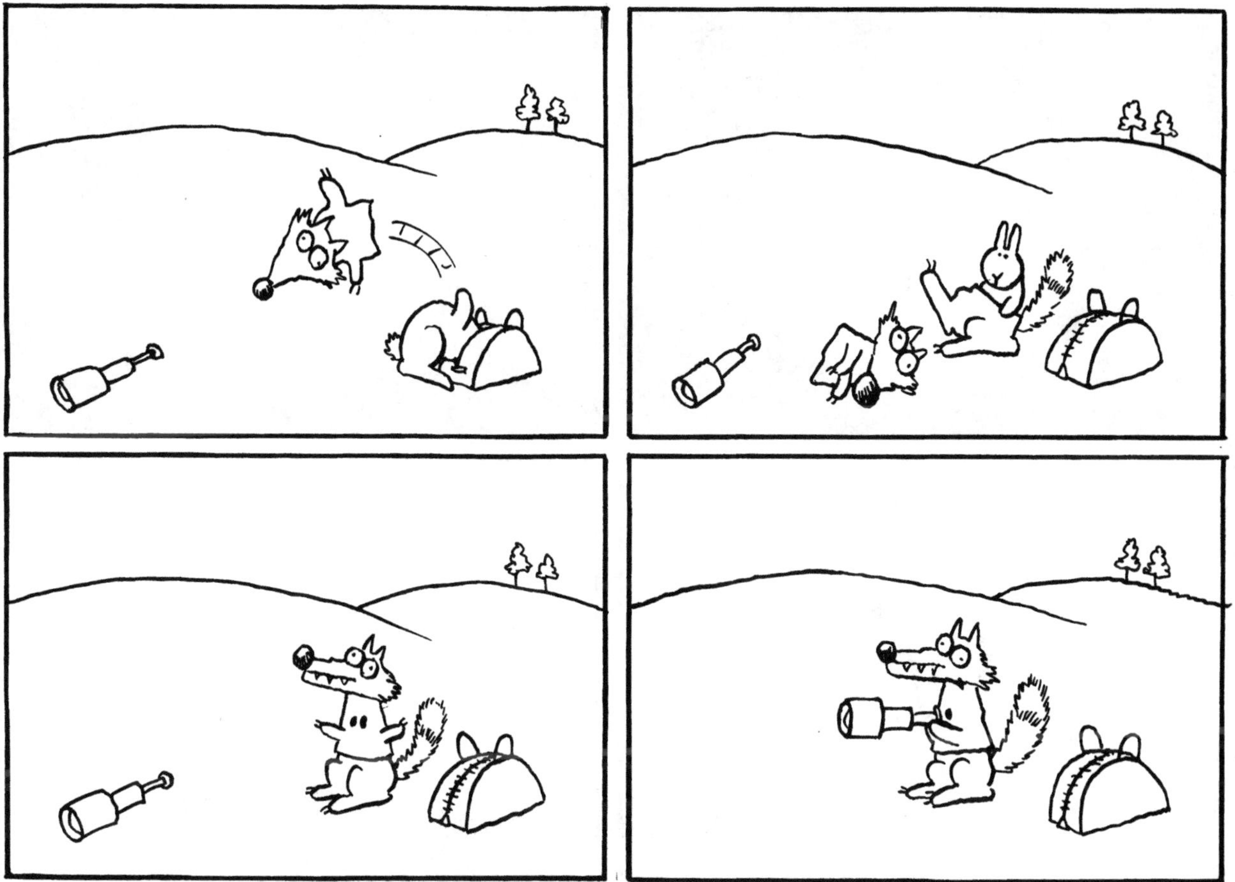

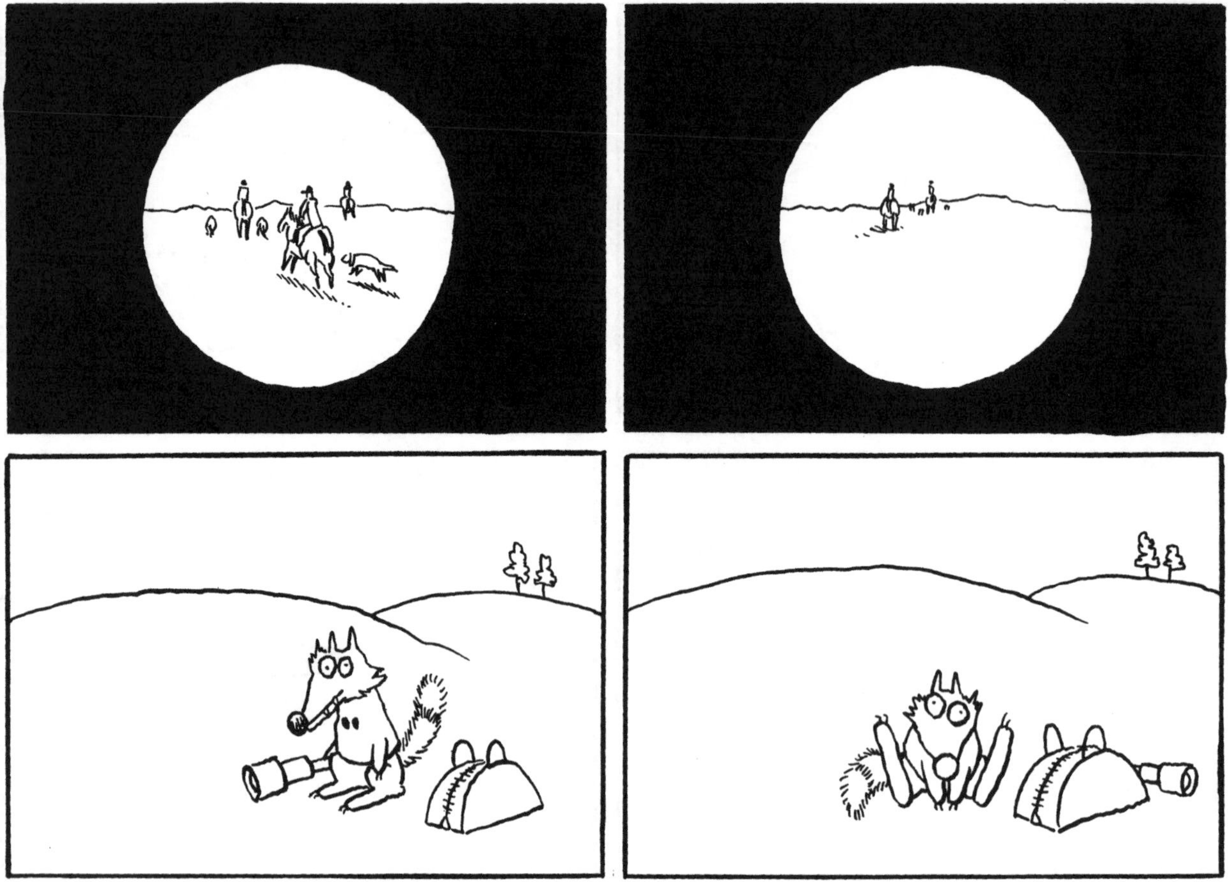

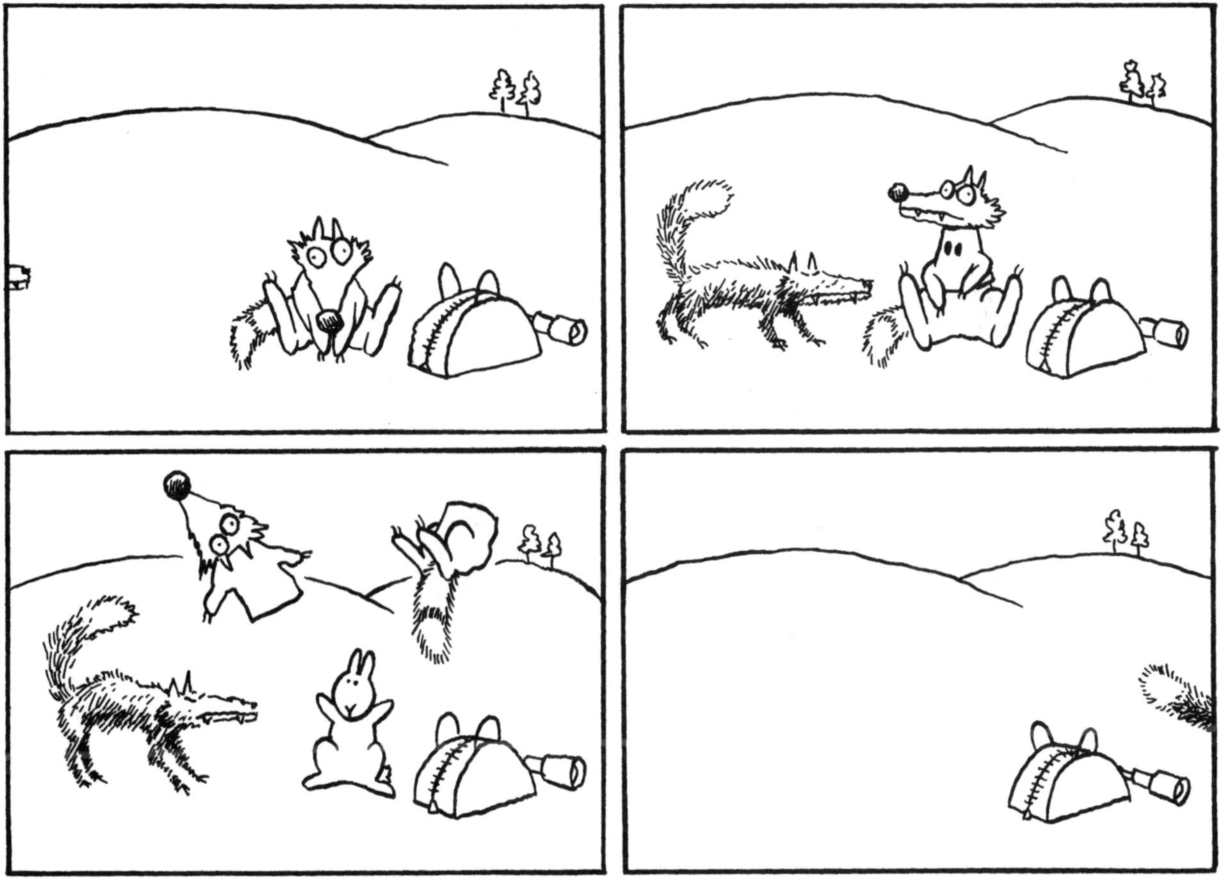

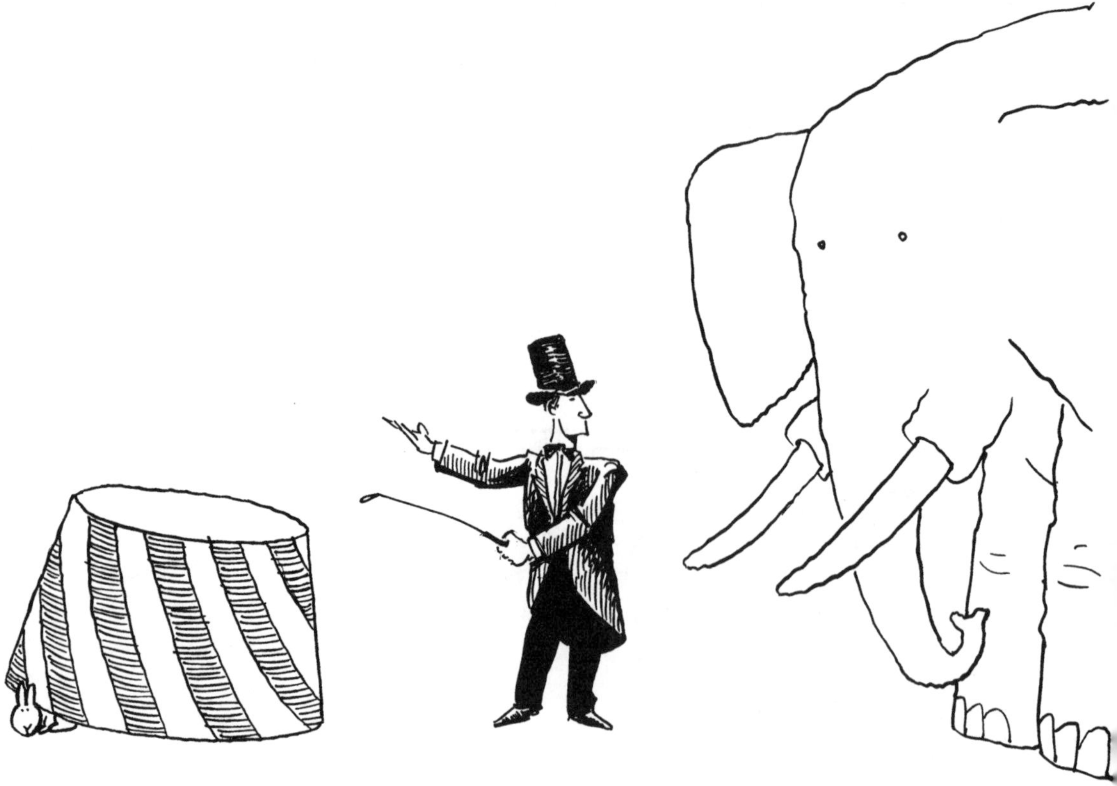

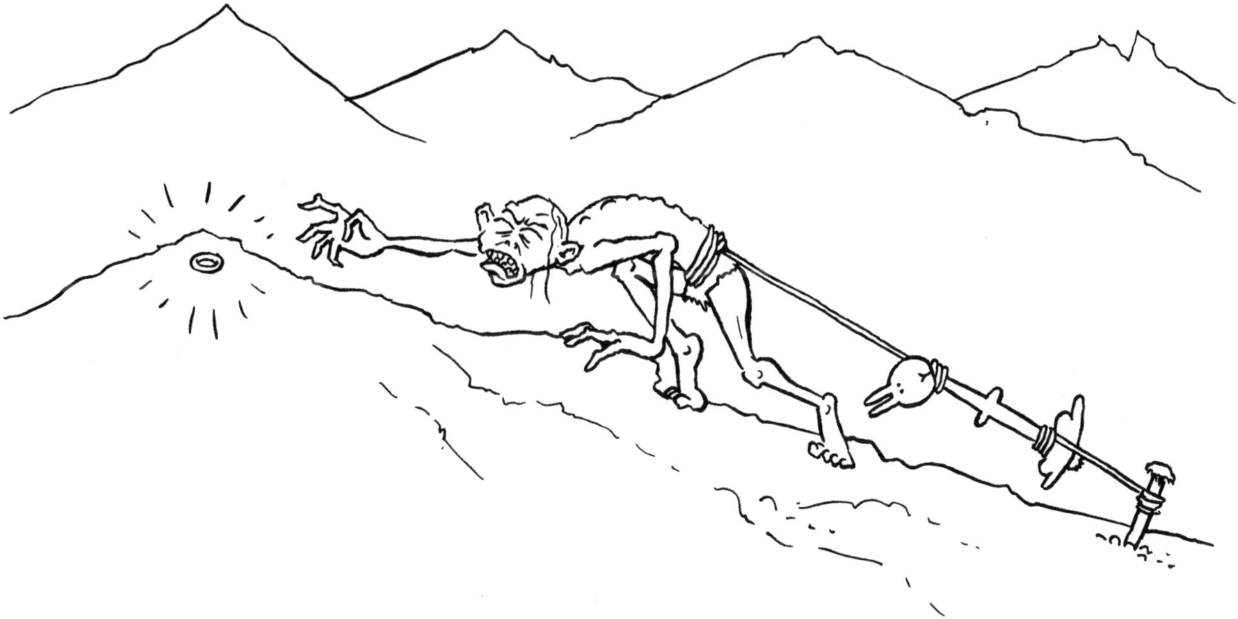

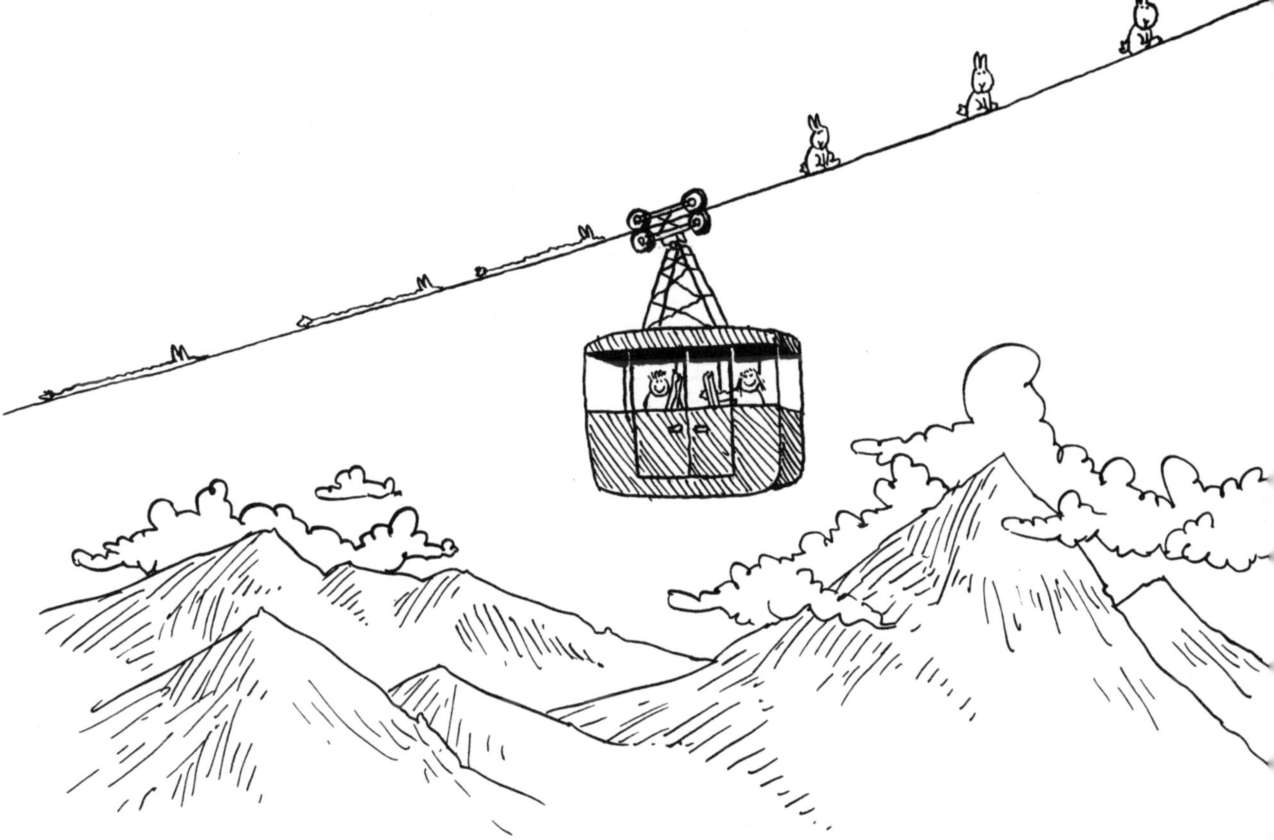

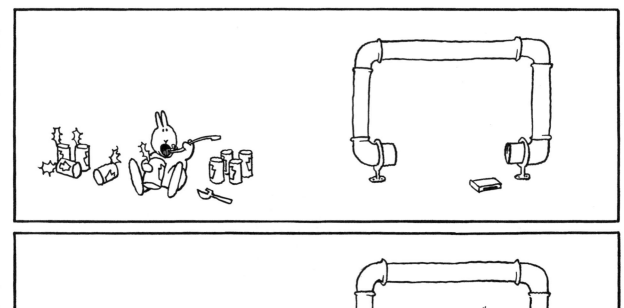
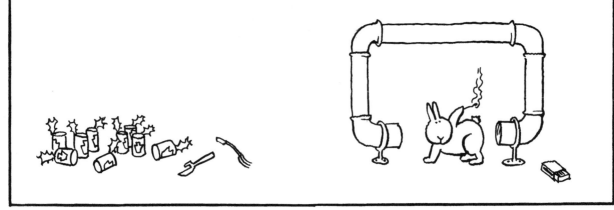

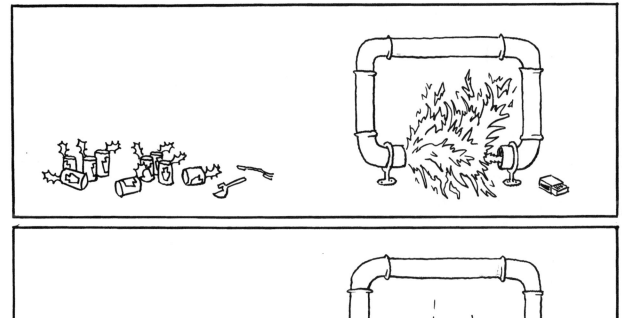
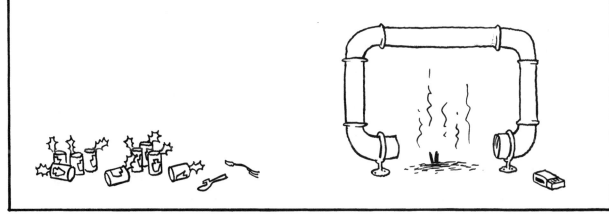

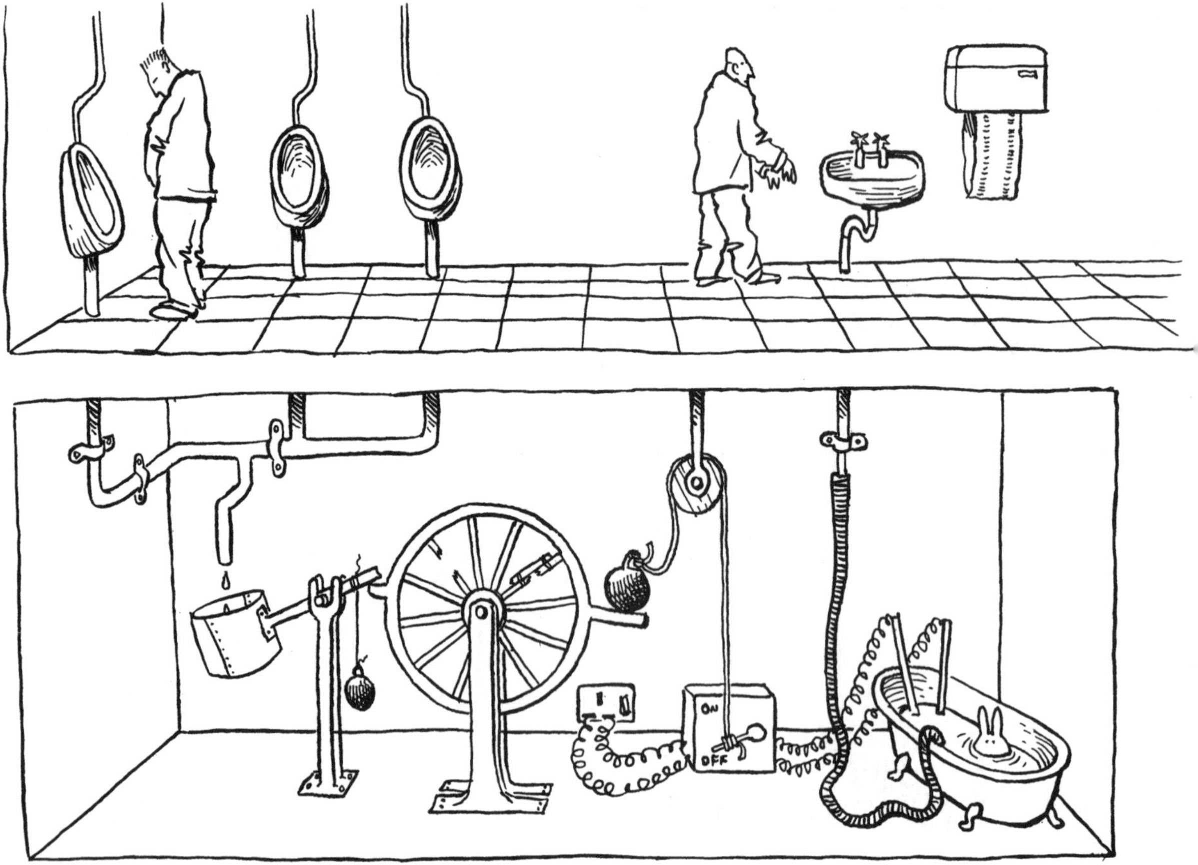
ON
OFF

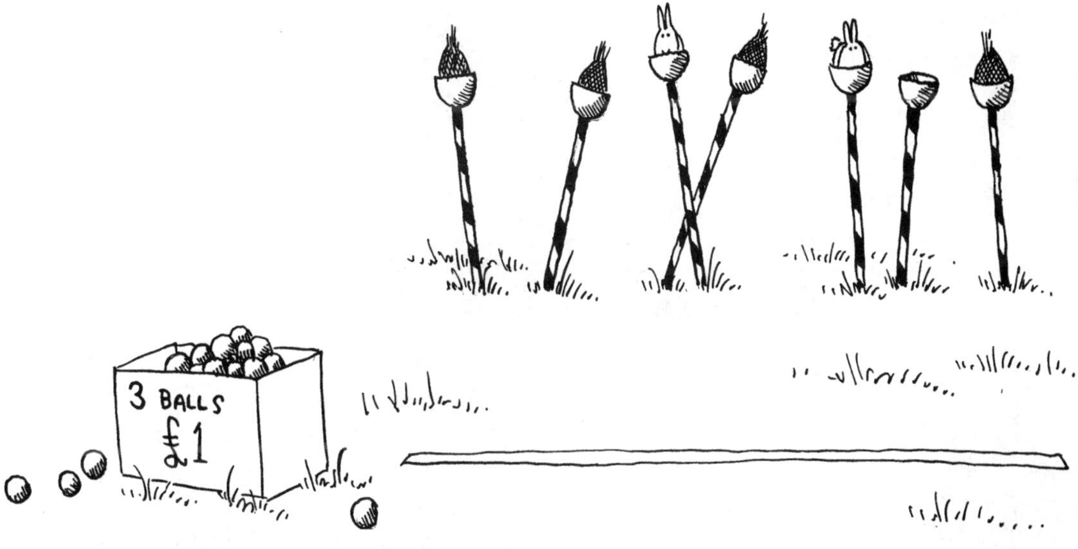
3 BALLS
£1

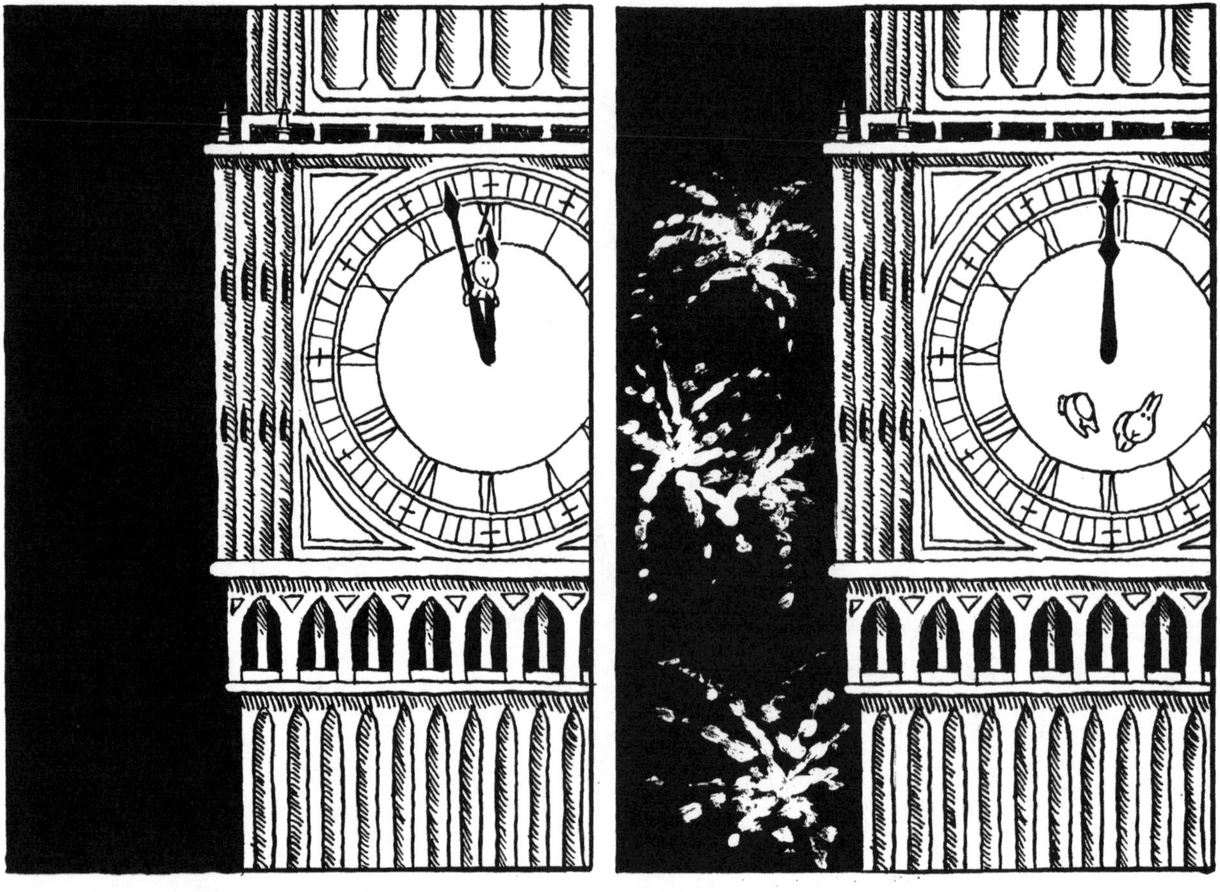

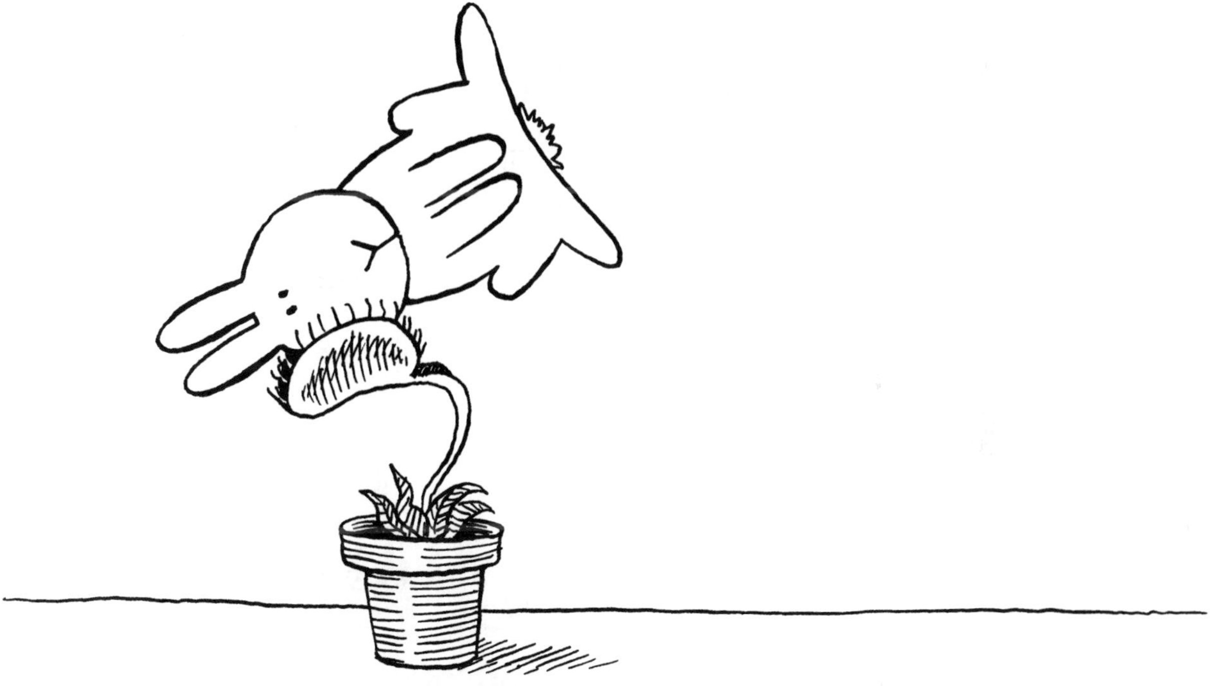

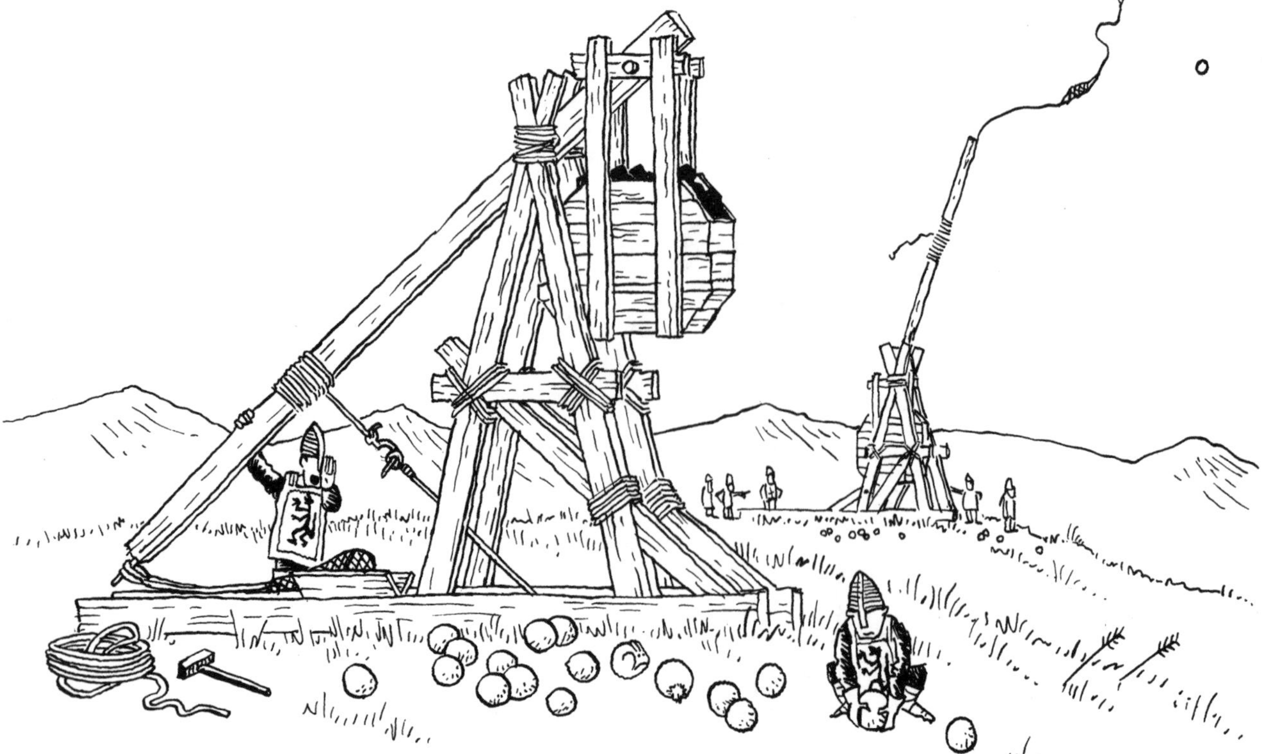

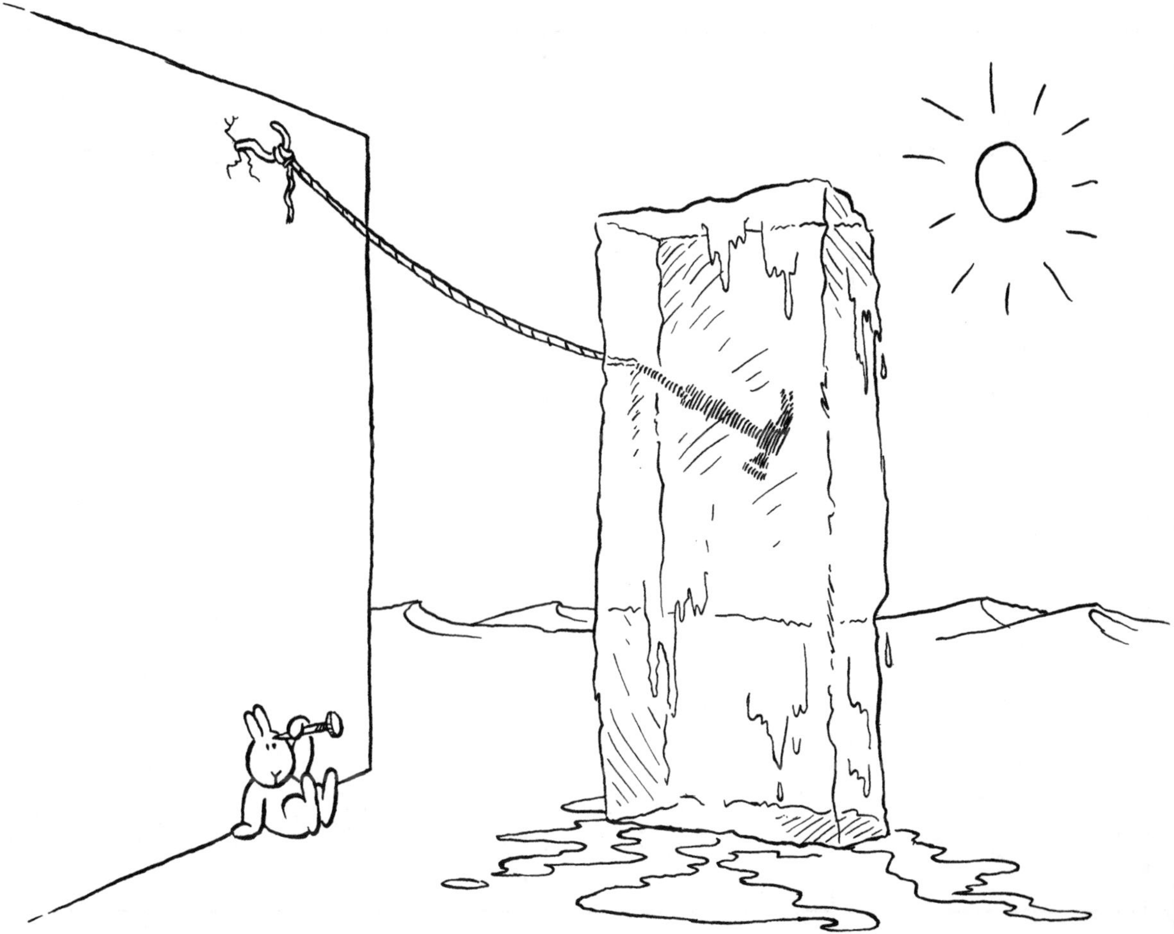

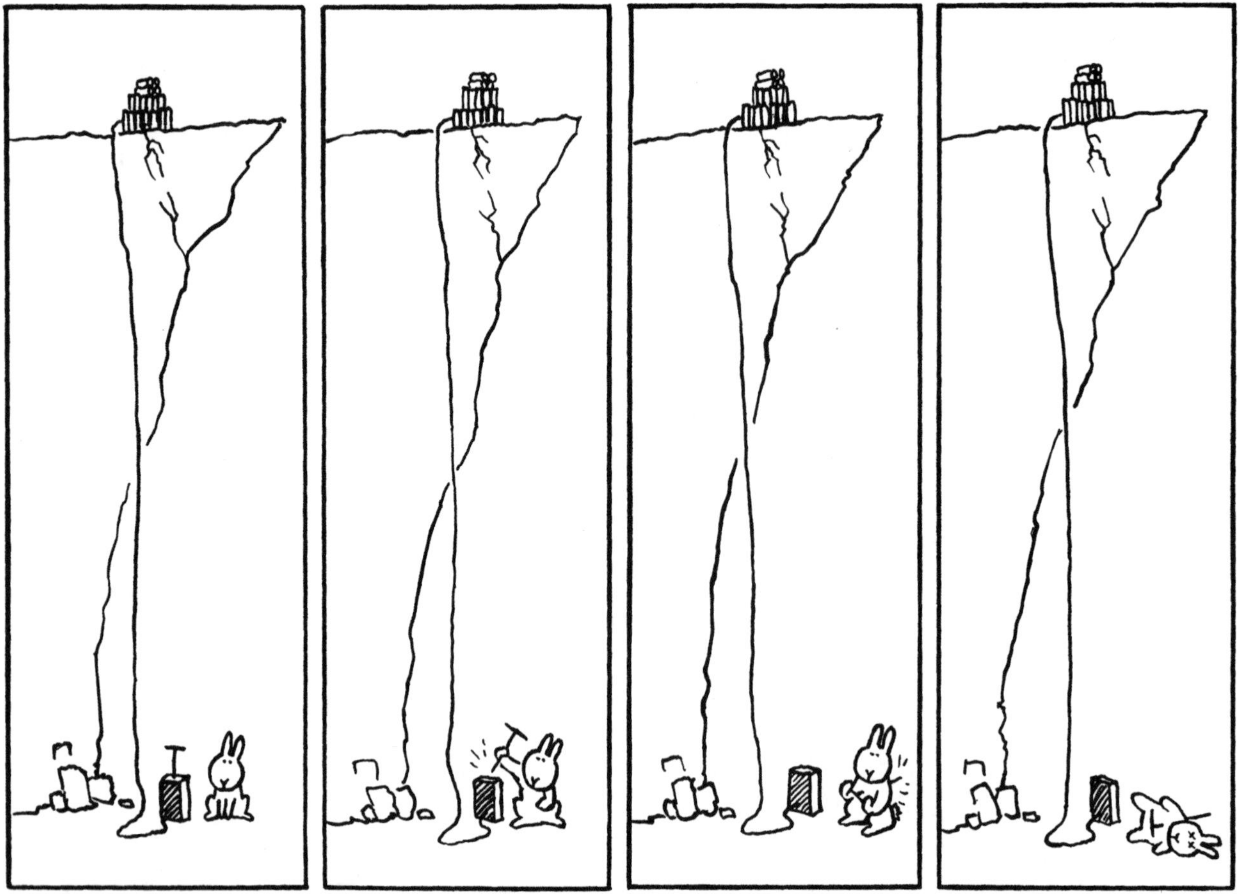

£01700
£1000
£100
£500
£300
£200
£1000
LOSE
£1000
£500
£100

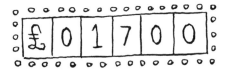

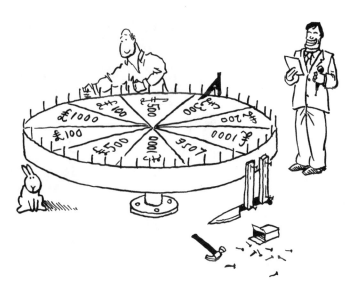

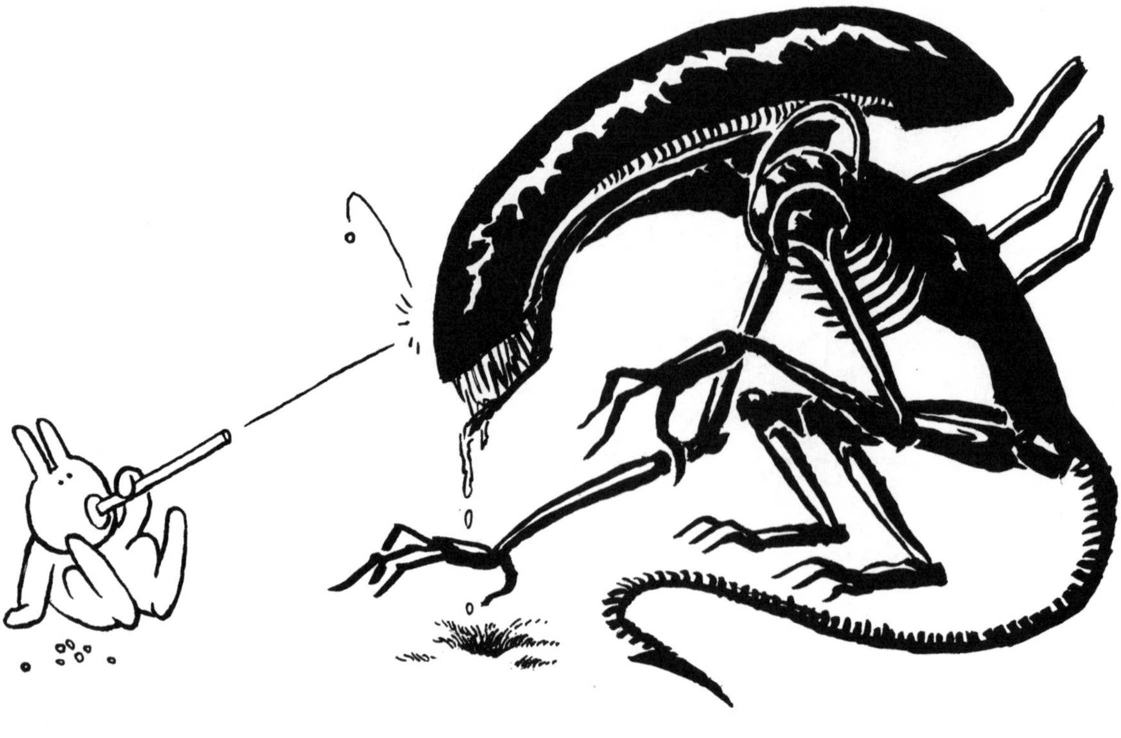

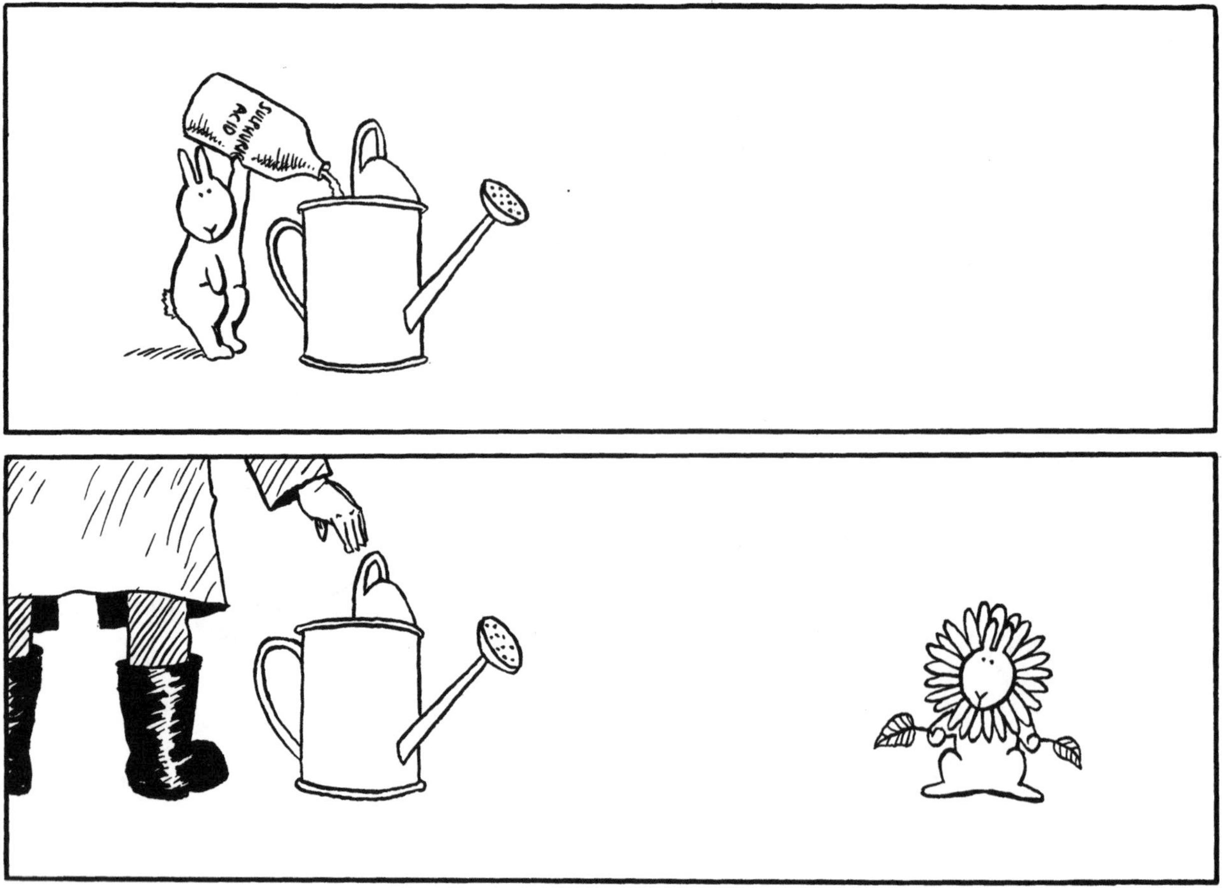
SULPHURIC ACID

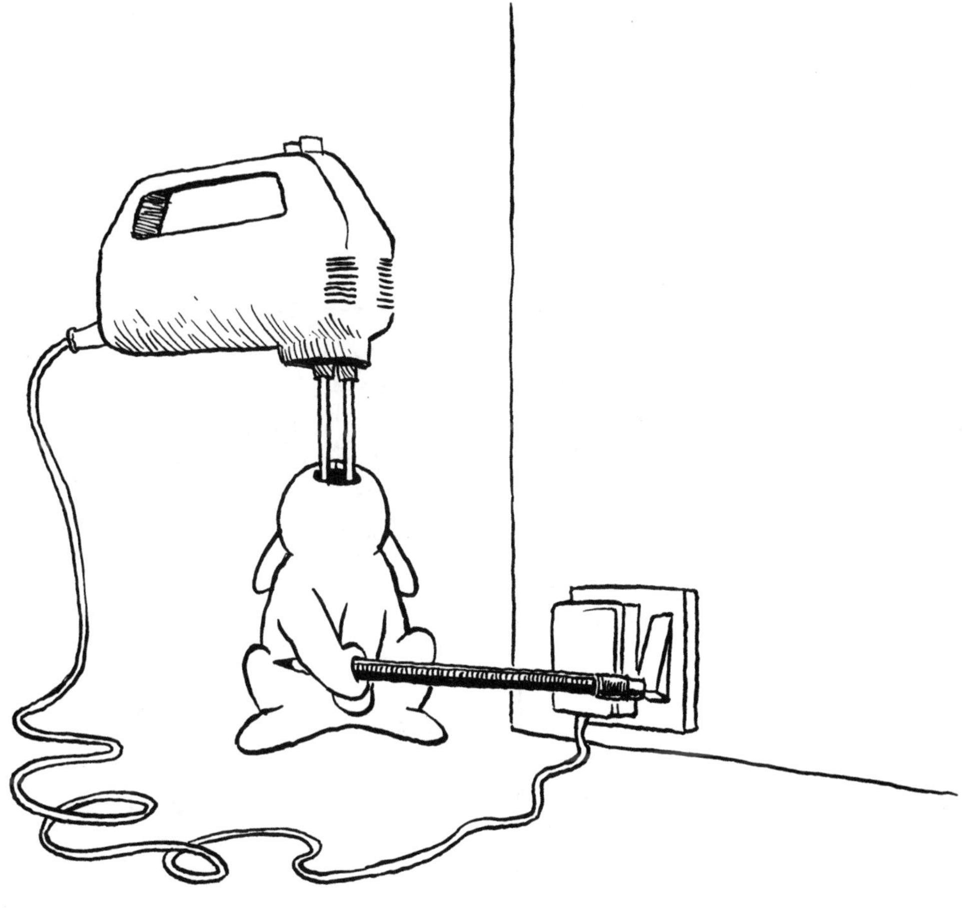

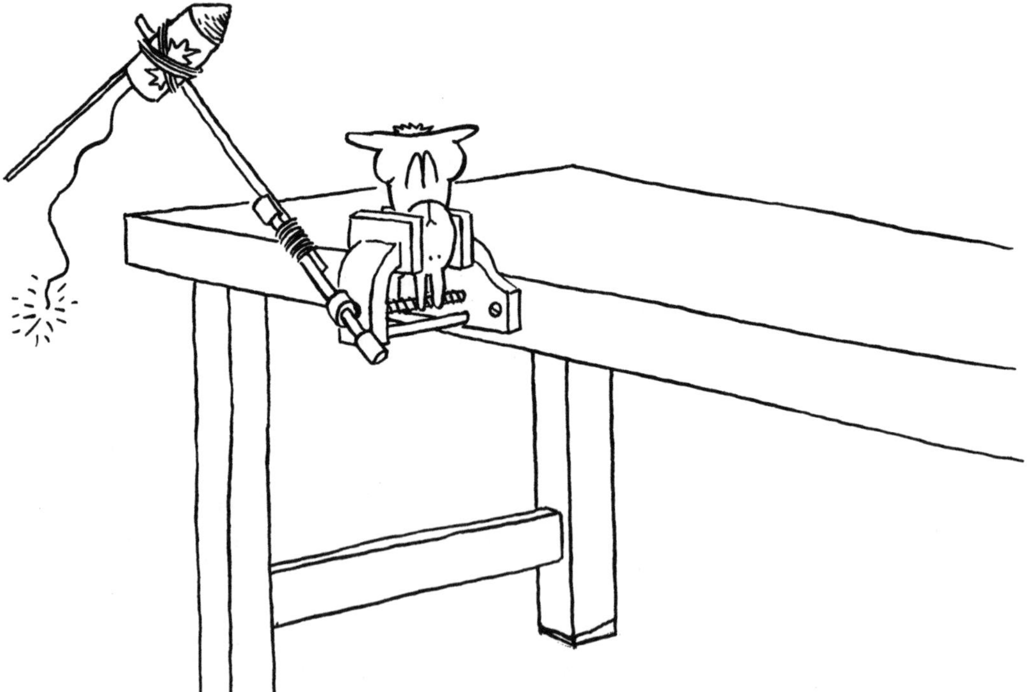

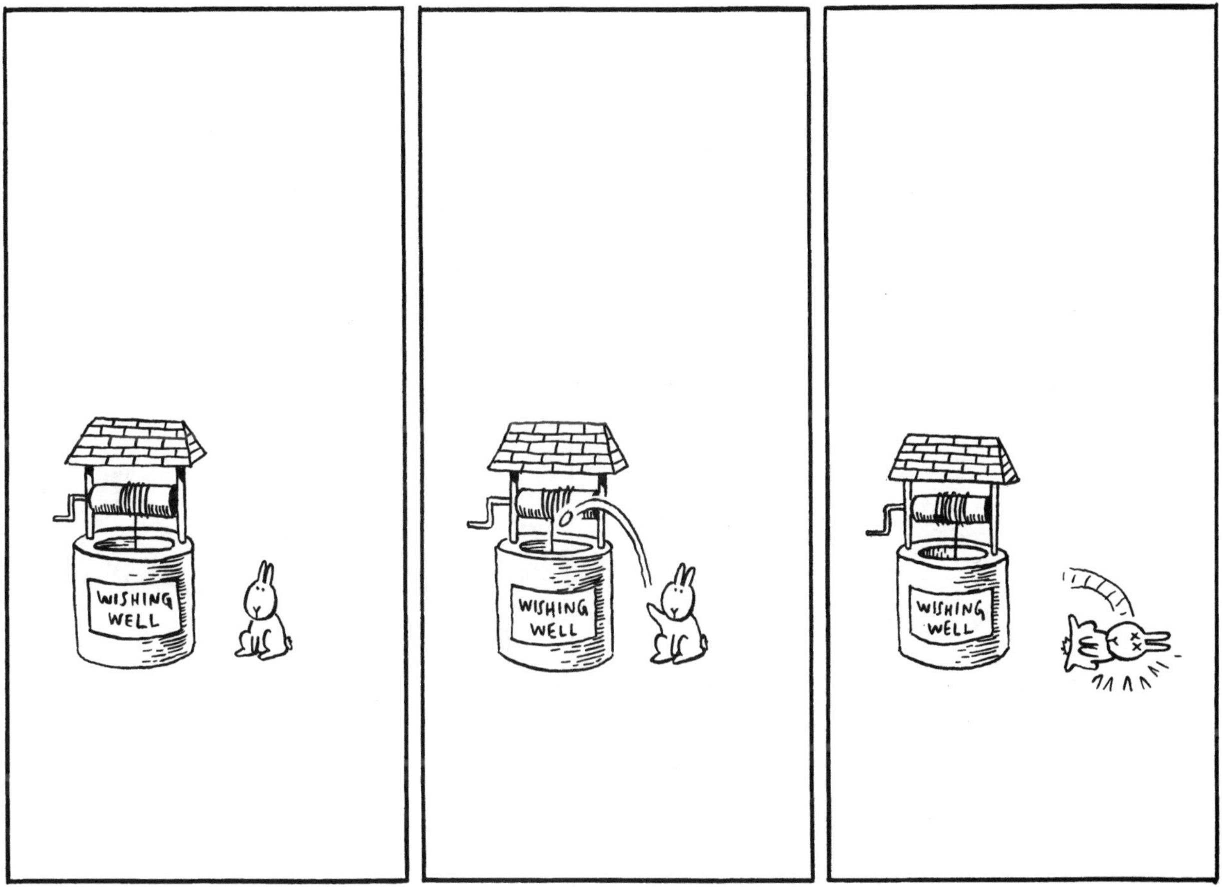
WISHING WELL
WISHING WELL
WISHING WELL

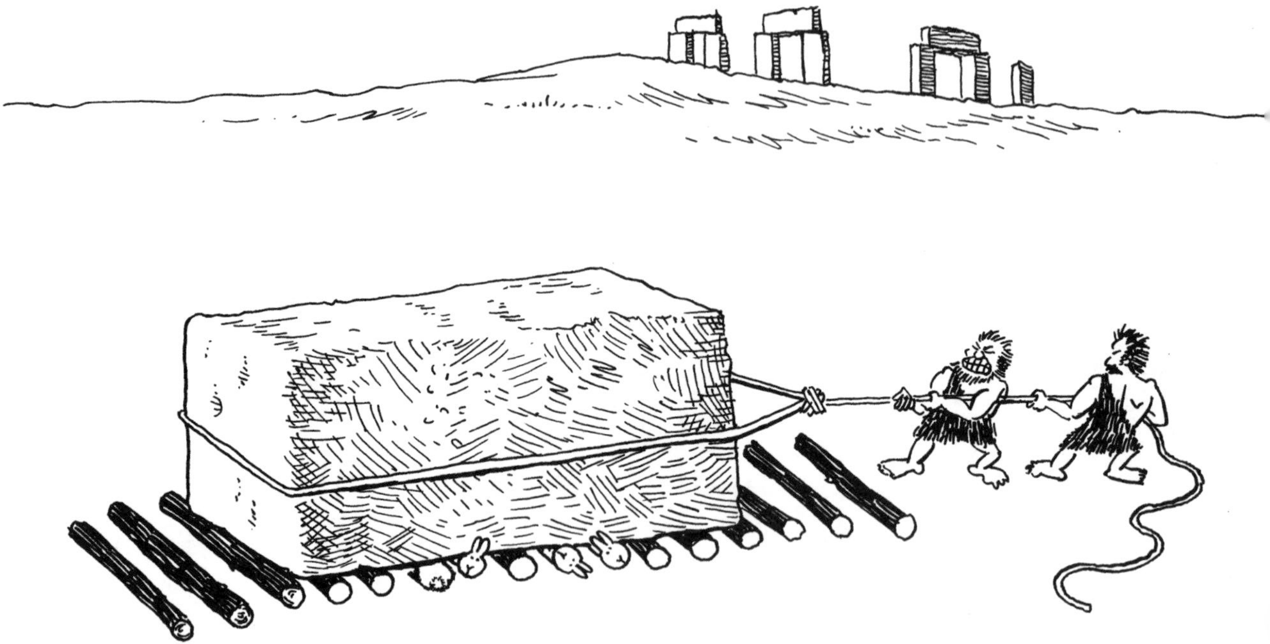

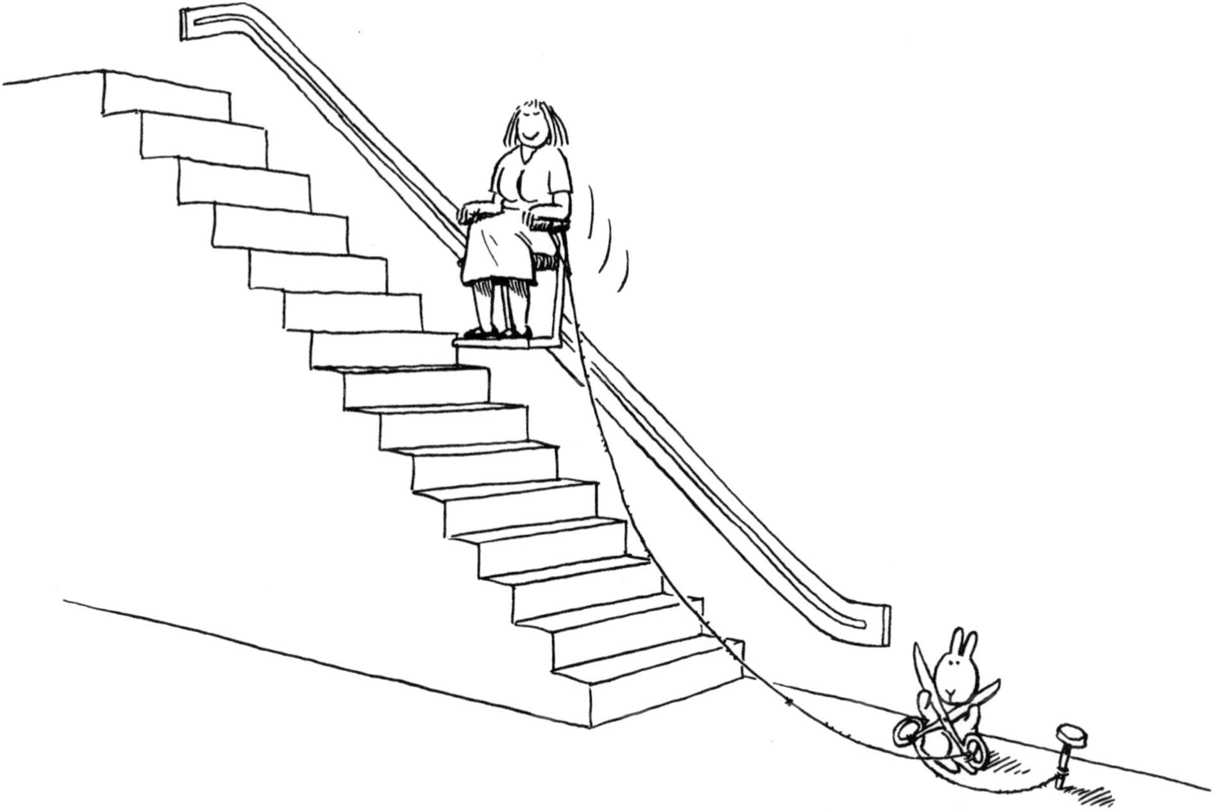

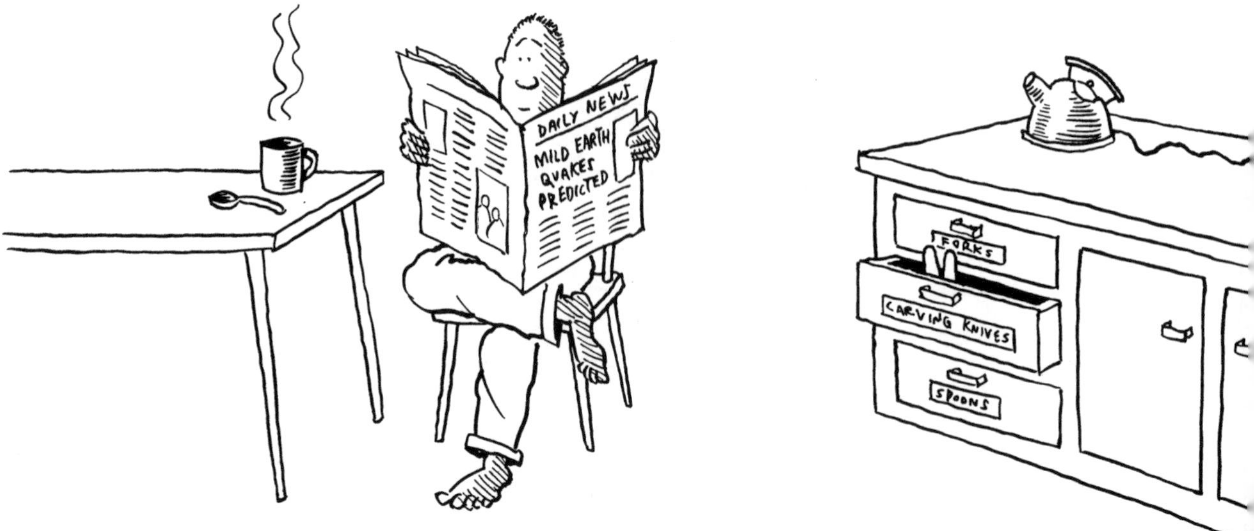
DAILY NEWS
MILD EARTH QUAKES PREDICTED
FORKS
CARVING KNIVES
SPOONS

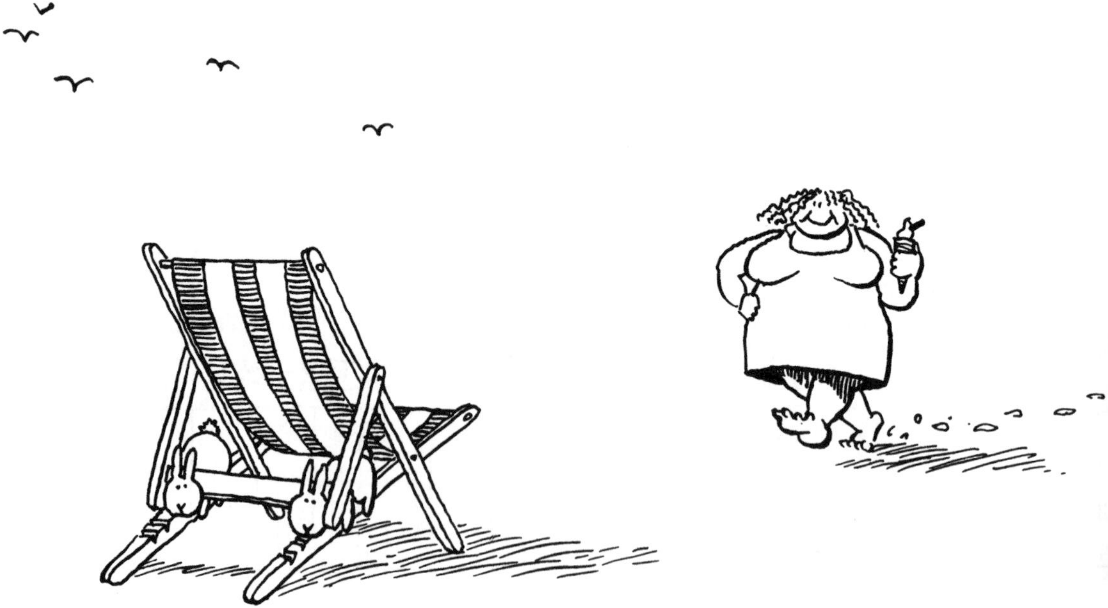

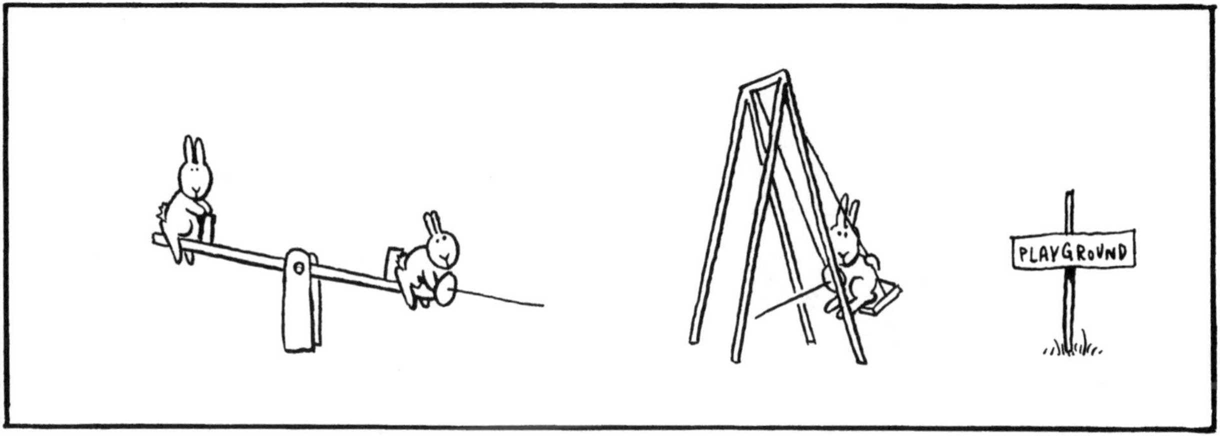
PLAYGROUND

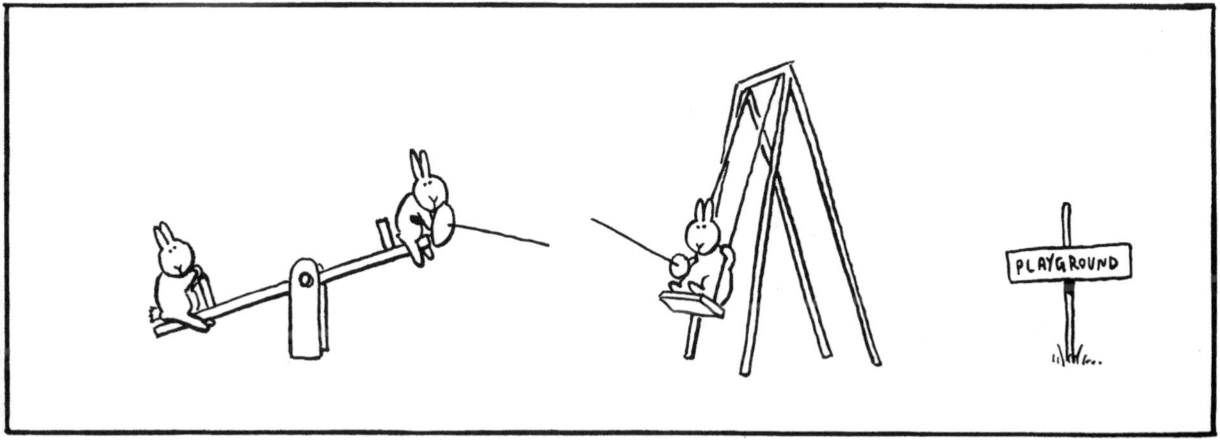
PLAYGROUND

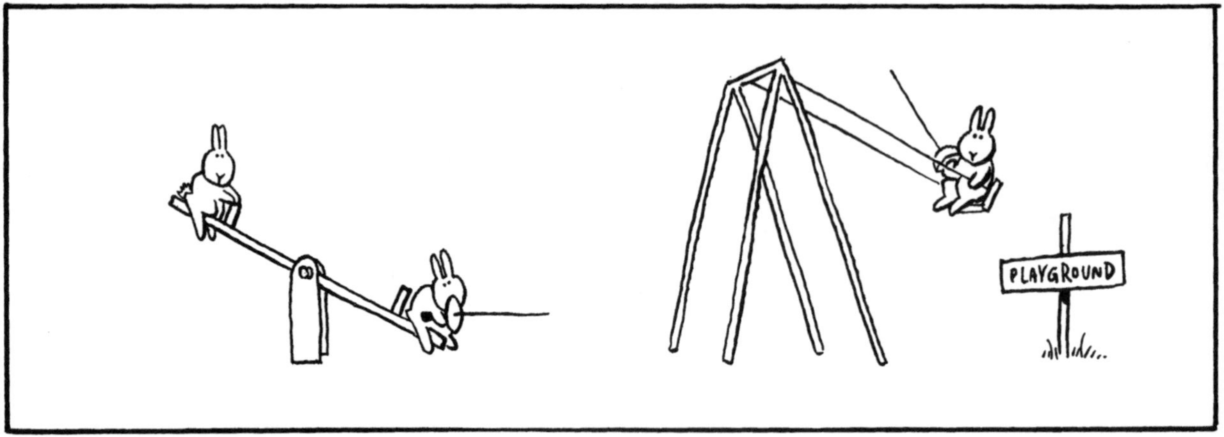
PLAYGROUND

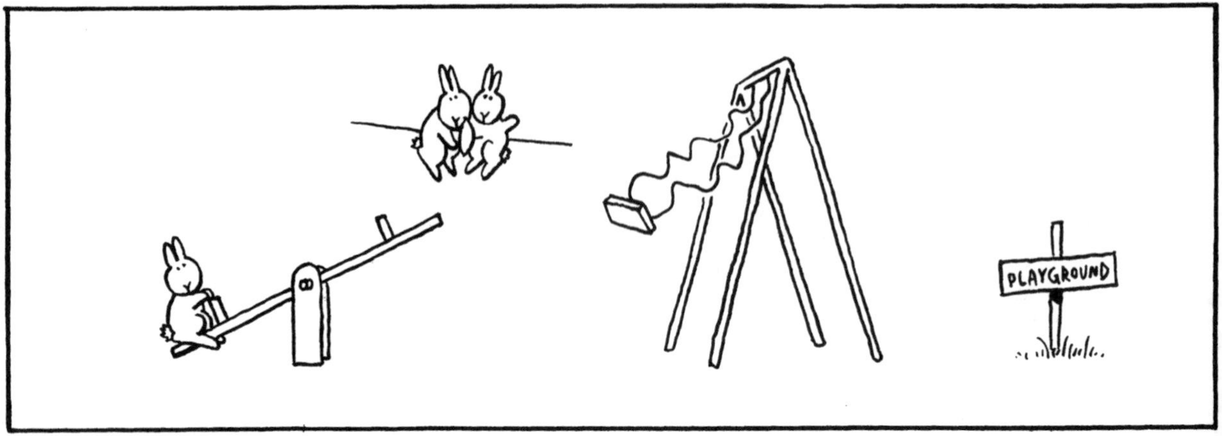
PLAYGROUND

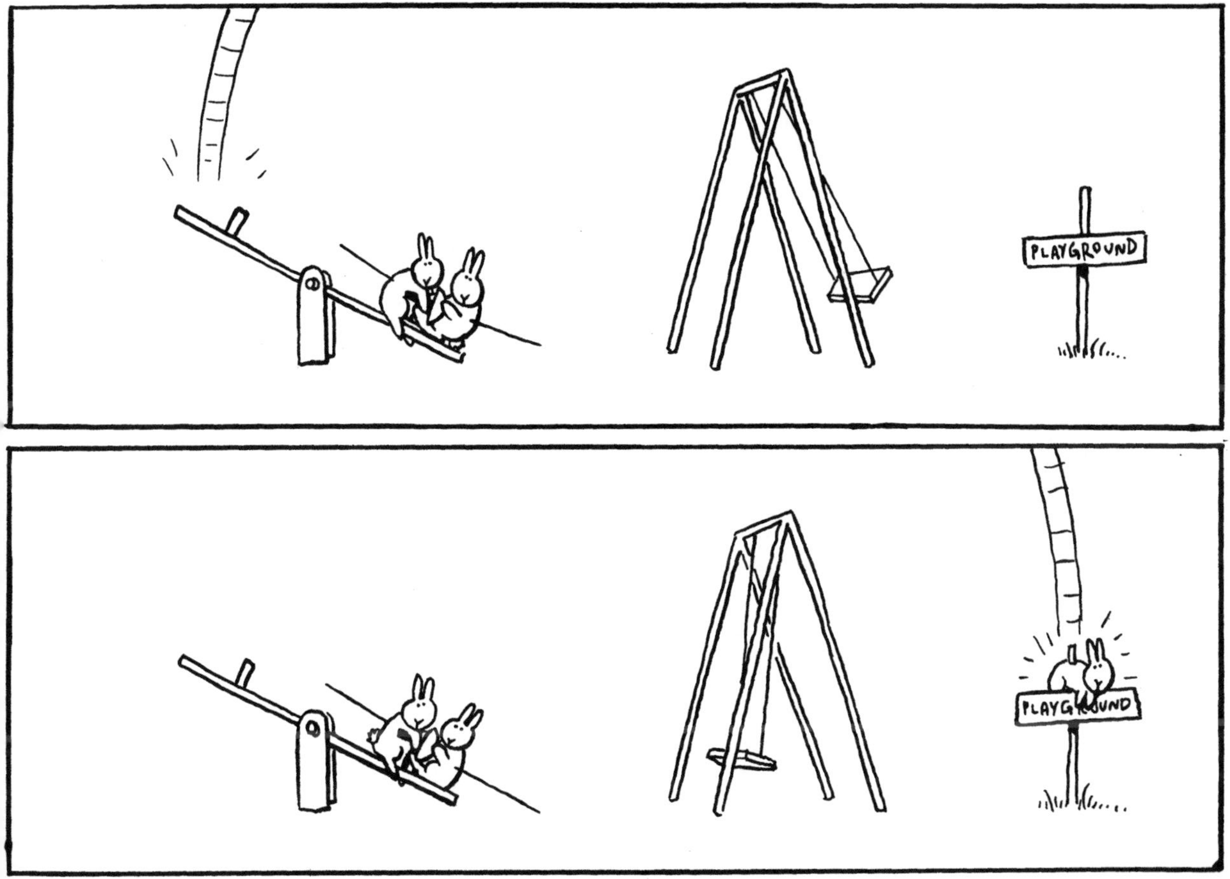
PLAYGROUND
PLAYGROUND

EPILOGUE

More Humor from the "Wonderfully Deviant"* Andy Riley

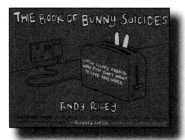

THE BOOK OF BUNNY SUICIDES
LITTLE FLUFFY RABBITS WHO JUST DON'T WANT TO LIVE ANYMORE
ANDY RILEY

978-0-452-28518-7

GREAT
!?
LIES To Tell
Small Kids
ANDY RILEY
FROM THE BESTSELLING AUTHOR OF THE BUNNY SUICIDES

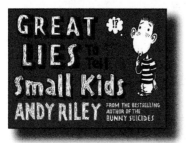

978-0-452-28624-5

Coming Soon!

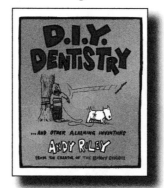

D.I.Y. DENTISTRY
...AND OTHER ALARMING INVENTIONS
ANDY RILEY
FROM THE CREATOR OF THE BUNNY SUICIDES

978-0-452-29003-7

BUNNY SUICIDES
ANDY RILEY
A POSTCARD BOOK

978-0-452-28703-7

LOADS MORE LIES
TO TELL SMALL KIDS
ANDY RILEY
FROM THE BESTSELLING AUTHOR OF THE BUNNY SUICIDES

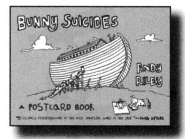

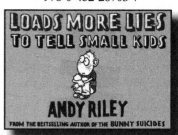

978-0-452-28856-0

* *The Washington Post*

Plume * A member of Penguin Group (USA) Inc. * www.penguin.com